The Hellenistic Age

A Captivating Guide to an Era of Mediterranean History That Took Place Between the Death of Alexander the Great and the Rise of the Roman Empire

Free Bonus from Captivating History (Available for a Limited time)

Hi History Lovers!

Now you have a chance to join our exclusive history list so you can get your first history ebook for free as well as discounts and a potential to get more history books for free! Simply visit the link below to join.

Captivatinghistory.com/ebook

Also, make sure to follow us on Facebook, Twitter and Youtube by searching for Captivating History.

Contents

Introduction

Over a span of just thirteen years (336 BCE to 323 BCE) Alexander the Great had led an empire-building campaign that sent ripples through many civilizations of the time. Greek culture and influence spread from Greece to India, leading to a new era, known as the Hellenistic age. The word "Hellenistic" stems from the ancient word *Hellas*, which is the original name of Greece. The term refers to speaking the Greek language or identifying with Greek culture and ideals.

The Hellenistic period starts with the death of Alexander in 323 BCE and ends in 31 BCE with the Roman defeat of the lands of the last Hellenistic kingdom. The Alexandrian Empire was a fragile one. It could not be solidified enough within thirteen years, and with the death of its leader, it was soon divided. Alexander's Diadochi (successors) eventually split the territories of the former empire into three different kingdoms: Macedon, the Seleucid Empire, and the Ptolemaic Kingdom. These territories would no longer be part of one empire; however, they still maintained a number of common Greek characteristics.

The three Hellenistic states represent the center of the Hellenistic age. Unlike the Greek city-states, they were not governed by the people. Instead of employing a democratic system, they became absolute monarchies. The new rulers shifted the focus of the kingdoms and brought a great deal of social, political, and economic changes to them. The main interest was developing highly successful commercial relationships throughout the old Alexandrian world. Spices, gold, and ivory were imported from India, linen and papyrus from Alexandria, oil from Athens, silver from Spain, and tin from Brittany. The successful trade led to the creation of imposing palaces and intricate sculptures, as well as the renowned libraries of Pergamum and Alexandria.

A new golden age of commerce and science began with the Hellenistic age. While the kingdoms were ruled separately, the people were united by a common tongue, known as Koine. This form of Greek allowed the culture and the people to stay united as they traveled freely between the new territories. However, a great number of citizens were not comfortable with their new way of life. Many of them were used to taking part in the decision-making process of the old city-states and contributing to the welfare of the people. Now, they suddenly felt dropped in the middle of a faceless kingdom governed by one authoritative figure and a new bureaucratic system.

The alienation of the people from the government and society itself can be seen as a result of the Hellenistic transformation. It can also be seen within the art of the period. Scholars, artists, and philosophers began rejecting the collective ideals, and instead, they focused on the cult of the individual. Sculptures were no longer that of gods and ideals but of individuals, and philosophers cultivated the ideas of individual happiness and pleasure. Religious cults, such as the cult of Isis, formed around the same concepts, claiming to offer the secret of immortality and prosperity to those who sought it for themselves.

The Hellenistic age brought a great deal of change in the ancient world. However, the era was destined to end in 31 BCE with the Battle of Actium. Octavian's Roman forces defeated Mark Antony's and Cleopatra's Ptolemaic fleet, thus securing the rise of the Roman Empire.

While the Hellenistic age lasted only for a brief period in humanity's rich history, its influence on culture, science, and philosophy has resonated with the world ever since.

Chapter 1 – The Beginning of a New Age

Timeline:

> 1. June 323: Death of Alexander the Great; the Lamian War begins
>
> 2. 322: Battle of Crannon and end of the Lamian War
> 3. 320: Death of Perdikkas; Antipater becomes regent

Alexander the Great died unexpectedly in 323 BCE in Babylon. The cause of his death is still unknown; however, malaria, typhoid fever, and poison have been speculated. Historians only agree on the fact that he died from a fever that lasted for ten days.

His generals, as well as the whole empire, were unprepared for this event. Out of the most influential men from his inner circle, only two of them were present that day. Ptolemy I Soter and Seleucus I Nicator debated the fate of the territories in the absence of the third future dynasty founder, Antigonus I Monophthalmus. Ptolemy was chosen to govern Egypt, while Seleucus was appointed to be the cavalry commander within the central government. Antigonus was still in Phrygia at the time, where he had been named governor by Alexander. In his absence, the two officers confirmed his appointment in order to avoid possible tensions and conflicts, as there was no real reason to replace him.

At this time, the biggest issue was establishing Alexander's successor. The gathering in Babylon faced a new debate. Alexander had a son called Heracles; however, he was still too young, and the king never recognized him. At the same time, Roxana, his first wife, was pregnant. In addition, Philip III Arrhidaeus, the other son of Philip II, Alexander's father and the former king of Macedonia, was still alive and present in Babylon; however, he suffered from some form of mental disability. So, the court reached an impasse. Every option they posed had a number of problems. In the end, the officers were under heavy military pressure from loyalist mutineers and declared Alexander's half-brother, Arrhidaeus, as the rightful heir. They also reached an agreement to name Roxana's child as a successor, should she give birth to a boy.

A few months after Alexander's death, a new male heir was born and named king. Both the mentally deficient brother and the young child, named Alexander IV, were unfit to rule; therefore, the true leader would be the regent, Perdiccas. At the same time, Antipater, another one of Alexander's generals, was reappointed in Macedonia. However, he was forced to govern together with Craterus, who, according to Alexander's orders, was supposed to be his successor. The other generals and influential officers were also given new titles and positions to fit their standing. For the time being, the command structure in the empire did not change fundamentally. The officers committed to their decisions in Babylon in order to maintain control and satisfy the army to avoid mutiny and chaos.

The first major problem facing Perdiccas was related to Alexander's burial. Everyone knew that his wish was to be buried in the oasis of Amun Ra (located in Siwa, Egypt) because of a spiritual experience he had when he entered the temple of Amun Ra. The problem with his dying request was that the prestige given by the tomb would go to Ptolemy instead of becoming a symbol for the Macedonian people. The royal line of Argead kings, the line of Alexander the Great's family, was buried in Macedonia (in the city of Aigai, now modern-day Vergina), where Antipater now upheld his rule. In either case, Perdiccas would lose support and prestige to one of his competitors, whether it was Egypt or Macedonia.

While the royal burial could be postponed for a while, the regent faced another major problem: maintaining unity in the imperial government. Where was the central power supposed to govern from? Perdiccas was appointed to his new function; however, he did not receive any territory. The regent may have been in charge of the empire, but Perdiccas knew that the new seat of power would influence the governor of its geographical location as well. In the end, he knew that he did not have a choice, as Macedonia was the traditional land of kings. He simply could not avoid facing Antipater. While possessing the corpse of Alexander the Great and the title of regent were two powerful advantages, they were also terrible burdens. Perdiccas faced the possibility of losing his role within the empire.

So, Perdiccas decided to form an alliance with Antipater by taking his daughter's hand in marriage. The betrothal would allow him to face Ptolemy from a position of consolidated power. However, Antipater was occupied with his own problems in Macedonia. Alexander's death emboldened the Aetolian League (a confederation of cities and tribes located in Aetolia, central Greece) and Athens to rebel against Macedonian rule. Between 323 and 322 BCE, this new alliance gathered an army to challenge Macedonian hegemony, laying siege to Lamia, Antipater's seat of power, in 322. The Siege of Lamia would give the war its name, the Lamian War, although it is also known as the Hellenic War.

Antipater needed allies to break the siege, so he sent for help from the other Macedonians. Craterus, his deputy, was already on his way from Babylon with a fresh army, and Leonnatus from Phrygia answered his call as well. At the same time, Athens attempted to use its good relations with Perdiccas to weaken Antipater's power base. However, Athens gained nothing from the attempt, as the plan was later discovered, and Demades, the leader of the Greek negotiations, was killed.

During the spring of 322, Leonnatus arrived near Lamia, but he died during the first battle against the Greeks. The siege was raised, and when Craterus reached the battlefield, the combined Macedonian forces managed to defeat the attackers. The Hellenic War ended with the Battle of Crannon in August 322 BCE. The result of this war led to significant changes within the social and political landscape of the Greek cities and communities. Macedonian rule became more involved with the inner workings of the local governments as Antipater insisted on separate negotiations and treaties. Every Greek participant was forced to accept the terms, except the Aetolian League, who managed to defend itself against the Macedonian forces due to its mountainous terrain.

Athens had lost its powerful fleet against the Macedonian forces in the Battle of Amorgos in the Hellenic War. As a result, the Macedonian forces set up a permanent military presence in the city. Athens was under Antipater's close supervision, so Macedonian influence became more powerful in the ancient city-state, especially due to the changes made to their constitution. Antipater revoked the citizenship status of the Greeks who owned less than 2,000 drachmas in wealth. Over 10,000 citizens lost their status and could no longer participate in the governmental process of their own community. Athenian democracy had finally ended, after surviving centuries of reforms and Spartan invaders.

It's worth noting that at the end of this conflict, three of the most valued Athenian personalities had been lost. The great general who united and managed the alliance of the Greek cities and tribal communities, Leosthenes, fell in battle. Hypereides, an orator who helped ignite the war within the Greek assembly, was executed by the Macedonians. Lastly, Demosthenes, the great orator who was responsible for the first Athenian resistance against Philip II, was hunted at the order of Antipater and committed suicide when he was cornered by the Macedonian forces.

Antipater's strategy in dealing with Athens placed a significant strain on the relationship between Macedonia and the rest of the

Greek city-states. His main purpose, so far, was to maintain Macedonian hegemony within the Alexandrian Empire, and he saw no alternative to changing the Athenian way of governing. The Hellenic War had shown him that the Greeks rejected Macedonian rule; therefore, Antipater had to implement certain measures to enforce his supremacy. The measures he took served to make Macedonian rule even more despised within the Greek regions.

Once Macedonian supremacy was reestablished, Antipater returned to Macedonia in order to further solidify his position within his own seat of power. He married his deputy's daughter, and he also offered his own daughter to Perdiccas. These personal alliances are a display of the importance of family relations within Macedonian political and social life, as personal relations still took precedence over governmental decisions.

As Perdiccas was about to take Nicaea, Antipater's daughter, as his bride, Alexander the Great's sister, Cleopatra, arrived to offer herself as an alternative. She and her family were no friends of Antipater; however, Perdiccas could not change his decision. Rejecting Antipater's alliance at this point would lead to a conflict between him and Macedonia. The regent still needed to establish the imperial seat of power, and he could not afford to make enemies of one of the most powerful governors.

At the same time in Egypt, Ptolemy solidified his power base. He successfully eliminated the deputy that was appointed from Babylon and extended his own influence farther than the territory he had been given. He annexed Cyrene without consulting the regent and built friendly relations with the kings of Cyprus. These events combined were enough to convince Perdiccas in 321 not to send Alexander's body to Egypt for burial. However, the regent failed to take Ptolemy as a serious threat.

Ptolemy maintained a close relationship with Arrhidaeus, one of Alexander the Great's generals who was in charge of Alexander's funeral procession. As soon as the embalmed corpse of the king arrived in Syria, Ptolemaic soldiers took over the transport and carried the body to Egypt. Alexander was to be buried in Memphis, where he had ruled over his territories. However, in order to achieve this coup against the regent, Ptolemy had to "cleanse" his own military forces from Perdiccas' loyal troops. They were placed there to prevent such an event from occurring, and Ptolemy's act would be that of clear defiance in the face of the imperial regent. Perdiccas was left with no other choice but to take military action in order to preserve his authority and the people's loyalty.

While Perdiccas' authority was endangered by Ptolemy's actions in Syria, there were other events taking place at the same time that equally eroded his influence. One of them occurred within the royal court where Arrhidaeus, Alexander's half-brother, was getting married. His betrothed, Eurydice, did not have the regent's approval. The situation was so grave that Perdiccas ordered the murder of the one who planned the alliance, her mother, Cynane. This action ignited a series of consequences within the court, as this affair was no simple family tragedy. Cynane was Alexander's half-sister, meaning that Eurydice was Philip II's grandchild. When the regent ordered the death of the bride's mother, it ignited a series of military revolts, forcing the regent's hand. Perdiccas had no choice but to accept the marriage and everything that came with it.

Perdiccas was threatened by another event as well; however, he was not alarmed at the time. Antigonus, who was earlier appointed to govern over Phrygia, refused to assist when Perdiccas was engaged in Cappadocia in 322. When the regent called him to court to explain his actions, Antigonus refused and joined Antipater in his campaign against what was left of the Aetolian League. When Antigonus reached Antipater, he claimed to have news about Perdiccas and his plans. He told the Macedonian leader that the regent had changed his mind and that he would be marrying Cleopatra. Antipater did not respond well to the news. He already had his own suspicions about Perdiccas, so he did not question Antigonus. All he knew was that the regent was in possession of Alexander's body and that he was escorting it with the old imperial army. Securing his power with marriage to Alexander's sister seemed feasible. This event is what sparked the cooperation between Ptolemy and Antipater.

Once the Hellenic War ended, the new alliance planned for an expedition to Asia Minor, which lasted from 321 to 320. During this short timeframe, several events occurred, and they were going to influence the future structure within the Macedonian government. The first event was the Battle of the Hellespont between Antipater's deputy, Craterus, and Eumenes, the governor of Cappadocia and Paphlagonia who was loyal to Perdiccas, in 321, which resulted in the death of Craterus. This event removed Antipater's personal problem of finding a suitable position for Craterus outside of his territories, as he could now gain complete dominion over Macedonia.

During the same year, Perdiccas advanced his troops into Egypt to punish Ptolemy for his actions. His invasion, however, did not go as planned. It was, in fact, a disaster, which began with the death of 2,000 men who drowned in the Nile during the crossing. With the repeated blows to his authority and the loss of troop morale, the officers led a successful mutiny and killed Perdiccas, sometime in 321 or 320. When the troops approached Memphis, the officers invited Ptolemy into their camp. He came with food and supplies, causing the demoralized soldiers to cheer for him. Soon, reports about the death of Craterus reached the troops. Eumenes, one of Perdiccas' most loyal followers, had been left in charge of the troops in Asia Minor; he was the one responsible for Craterus' fall in battle. The remaining troops condemned his actions and sentenced him to be executed. However, Ptolemy avoided any kind of responsibility for any of these actions, and he escorted the dead regent's armies back to Syria. The defeated troops gathered in Triparadisus, where they joined forces with Antipater. There it was decided that Antipater should take the mantle of imperial regent, following Perdiccas' tragic end.

Antipater's new function allowed him to establish the center of Macedonian rule back to Macedonia. Unlike Perdiccas, he had no interest in Asia Minor. He had already reached an old age by this point and desired to focus solely on the Macedonian territories. Another important decision taken at Triparadisus was to maintain Ptolemy's control of Egypt. He proved more than capable of defending it, and Antipater offered him one of his daughters as his new bride.

Even though Perdiccas was dead, his loyal supporter, Eumenes, remained a threat to the new order. He governed from Cappadocia, which was the heart of a vital trading network that spread throughout Anatolia. Antipater, however, had to wish to eliminate this new resistance. Antigonus, on the other hand, offered himself as a solution to the Perdiccas problem. He governed the territories that bordered Cappadocia, so he was given charge to handle the threat due to his knowledge of the land. Antipater rewarded Antigonus with the title of General of Asia and forged the alliance with family blood, as tradition demanded. He offered his daughter, Phila, the late Craterus' wife, to Antigonus' son, Demetrius. Four decades later, this betrothal would lead to the naming of a new king of Macedonia.

The final discussion at Triparadisus was about the reward that was to be given to the officers who led the rebellion against Perdiccas. There were two key leaders that played a vital role in the former regent's death. One was Seleucus, the man in command of the imperial cavalry, and Antigenes, who commanded the guards. Seleucus was named satrap (governor) of Babylonia and Antigenes satrap of Susiana. Both of these appointments were planned by Antipater, as he wanted the men to be as far away from him as possible in order to avoid any kind of future conflicts of interests.

Chapter 2 – Cassander, Rise of a New King

Timeline:

1. 319: Death of Antipater; Polyperchon becomes regent
2. 317: Olympias returns to Pella in Macedonia; death of Arrhidaeus and Eurydice
3. 316: Cassander returns to Macedonia; death of Olympias

After Antipater's successful negotiations at Triparadisus in 321, he returned victorious to his seat in Macedonia, bringing the royal court with him. A traditional governing system had been reestablished back in Macedonia, which became the center of the Argead dynasty once more. The other territories recognized the central power and agreed to depend on Macedonian troops and governmental rulings. Local governing positions could only be named by the central authorities, and the surrounding states were obligated to transfer a percentage of their wealth to Macedonia. Antipater moved Perdiccas' treasury to the new court and transferred enough funds to Antigonus so that he could pay for his military expedition against Eumenes.

Everything seemed to go as planned for Antipater. Unfortunately, he was eighty years old, and he would die sometime in the next year, unable to see his plan come to fruition. If he had, he would've created a separate European and Asian territory. Antigonus would have taken responsibility for the Asian territories while recognizing Macedonia as the incontestable power. Of course, this plan depended on Antigonus' ability to defeat Eumenes.

Antipater died in 319 BCE, and no one else was there to fill his shoes. He enjoyed power, prestige, and authority like few kings had before him. He served as King Philip II's right-hand man during the battles for dominance against the Greeks and later governed Macedonia under Alexander the Great as he pushed to carve out an empire. With this kind of prestige and leadership skills, Antipater stayed in his highly regarded position due to the support of the people and the army. Unfortunately, in Macedonia, prestige and reputation could not be transferred to an heir. This aspect of governing combined with Antipater's loyalty to the royal house of kings pushed him to choose someone other than his son as his successor.

Antipater was loyal to Arrhidaeus and the newborn king, Alexander IV; however, neither of them was prepared to rule a kingdom. Antipater's loyalty to the royal house also prevented him from creating the image that he was trying to take the crown. He feared that naming his eldest son, Cassander, as the new regent would infuriate many influential people. Therefore, he appointed Polyperchon to become the next regent instead. He was an old man, but as someone who served the royal house of Macedonia and as someone who had followed Antipater for years, he would share the same ideals. Polyperchon served under Alexander the Great as a loyal officer, fought in the Hellenic War alongside Craterus, and governed Macedonia when Antipater was absent. In Antipater's mind, he was the perfect choice to be accepted by both the troops and the royal houses.

Cassander was to become Polyperchon's right-hand man. He was in his late thirties when his father passed. Cassander, however, had never served under Alexander the Great. He stayed close to his father in Macedonia and supported him in his struggle against the family of Olympias. He also represented him in Babylon, even though he wasn't welcome there. When Alexander died, Cassander was present, and he witnessed firsthand how the officers and generals were conspiring to carve their own wealth from the empire. For a short time, he served under Antigonus as his righthand, but he had to return home due to Antipater's bad health.

Another clear example of family relations and personal interests taking precedence can be seen here. During the times of Philip and Alexander, a tradition of loyalty to the Macedonian royal house was cultivated. However, the current representatives were rarely present in the lives of the people and the troops. They planned, schemed, and ruled within the walls of their courts. The traditional loyalty of the military was slowly dissipating, and the troops even noticed that each commander was in charge of paying a group of soldiers. This responsibility used to fall to the king. Now, the troops were being paid to serve the personal ambitions of their commander.

This erosion became even more prominent than before when Cassander became concerned about the new role he was about to play. Polyperchon wasn't as well respected and loved by the newer generation of soldiers, and since Cassander was not pleased with his father's decision, he formed a plan to seek aid from the military commanders that were stationed in the Greek cities, as well as from Ptolemy and Antigonus. They responded and offered him military help, which included a number of ships as well. With this act, Cassander declared his dismissal of Polyperchon's appointment as regent. With Antigonus on his side, this would mean civil war throughout the empire if Polyperchon decided to take arms against them.

Antigonus maintained the impression that he wanted to respect the agreement he made with Antipater, as he made assurances that he still wished to govern over a divided Asian empire and that he would continue to respect the authority of Macedonia. He still supported Antipater's vision; however, he wasn't happy with Polyperchon as his choice for regent. However, Antigonus agreed with Cassander when it came to hereditary rule. Neither of them had any problem when it came to the idea of creating a line of regents to rule Macedonia.

Polyperchon, on the other hand, faced a dilemma that could shatter the empire. He was loyal to Antipater and accepted his appointment, but he was now against the regent's son. He knew this situation could lead to a divided land, and he didn't know whether Antipater's own troops would stay on his side.

In 318, Antigonus openly showed that he stood for Cassander. He confiscated a transport fleet that was carrying around twenty tons of silver from Asia to Macedonia. Polyperchon knew that he had no choice but to rely on the Greek cities for commerce and troops. However, he did not know whether the garrison commanders that were appointed to supervise over the Greek cities were on his side. Nonetheless, Polyperchon had to stay in control of the Greeks, even if it seemed impossible.

Polyperchon was facing two major problems at this point. He could not risk replacing Cassander's royal commanders as this act could cause an open conflict. In addition, the commanders might simply refuse his orders. The second problem stemmed from the changes that Antipater made to the constitutions of every single Greek city-state. Loyal, wealthy men were appointed within the local governments, and they had prospered as a result of it. Polyperchon argued that those men would stay loyal to the son of the regent who brought wealth and prosperity into their lives and that there was little chance of them supporting Polyperchon.

In Macedonia, he also found himself severed from any political support. He could not benefit from the alliances and connections that Antipater made during his reputable lifetime, so his only choice was to enlist aid from Alexander's mother, Olympias, who had been removed from her seat in Macedonia by Antipater.

Antipater's death had led to a battle for supremacy. In European Macedonia, Cassander had to race against Polyperchon in order to gain the support of the Greek city-states and Macedonian garrisons. No territory would be able to escape the struggle between the two. In the Asian territories, Antigonus began a similar campaign for the support of the people. He was experienced in freeing cities from Persian domination as he had led several successful campaigns in the area while he served under Alexander. This experience proved to be invaluable as it gave him insight into each city's unique system of governing and population. Antigonus understood the people from the Asian-Greek cities and was even sympathetic to their involvement in the struggle between the Macedonian lords; however, he had to bring them under Cassander's influence.

At the same time, Polyperchon's court welcomed a large number of official representatives from the Greek cities. They came to seek answers from the regent and to receive guarantees from him. However, Polyperchon knew that the men came to assess the political situation in order to make a decision. Who were they going to support, the chosen regent or Antipater's son? Cassander had already placed his own loyal garrison commander in Athens without any interference, so Polyperchon assumed that most of the cities that prospered from Antipater's constitutional changes would side with Cassander as well, making his options rather limited.

Polyperchon had one choice, and it was a risky one. He issued a royal decree in the name of the king to restore the democratic constitutions which the Greek cities enjoyed before the Hellenic War. He allowed the ousted exiles who lost their citizenship to return to their cities. With this move, Polyperchon hoped to embolden the opposition to be on his side. This decision, however, made enemies of the Greeks and Macedonians who profited from Antipater's revised constitutions. The locals feared the social, economic, and political implications that such a drastic change would bring. In the spring of 318, Polyperchon traveled with Arrhidaeus to the Greek cities in order to spread his influence further. His goal was to push his propaganda to solidify his relationship with the democratically restored cities.

Polyperchon's decree was most resounding in Athens, the city which arguably suffered the most from Antipater's reforms. Democracy was restored to the ancient city-state, and the regent's army was nearby to ensure security. The new democratic leaders, emboldened by the military protection from Polyperchon, began a campaign against everyone who benefitted from Antipater's rule.

The Athenians were quite unforgiving. One of the most notable people who fell victim to the restoration was Phocion. He was a prestigious character known to be just and incorruptible, and he served Athens faithfully for nearly five decades. However, he made the mistake of maintaining his position as *strategos* (a military governor) under Antipater as well. The Athenians could not forgive him, and his reputation was not enough to protect him. He was executed at the order of the new government assembly. This is only one example of the chaos that ensued as the result of Polyperchon's decree.

Unfortunately for Polyperchon, his plan wasn't as successful as he had hoped. The constitutional changes brought even more instability and division to the Greek and Macedonian states. Many cities delved into chaos, just like Athens had. Cassander took full advantage of the situation and gathered a greater number of allies from those who were attacked by the regent's decree.

Later that year, Cassander arrived at the Macedonian garrison that was still present in Athens. He brought with him a fleet that he was given by Antigonus. Taking advantage of the political division that had occurred in Athens, he employed Demetrius of Phalerum, one of his local supporters, to be his new governor. Demetrius had survived the Athenian purge, and with his help, Cassander was able to gather more supporters to his side. Before the restoration, he lowered the citizenship requirements set by Antipater. To be a citizen, one used to have to possess 2,000 drachmas, but Cassander imposed a requirement of 1,000 drachmas instead. Other cities joined his cause soon after.

Polyperchon became increasingly unpopular in the Greek cities because he had enforced the new decree with his own army. This meant that as he traveled, the cities had to accommodate a large number of troops at their own expense. The regent's campaign for the support of Greece lasted for several years, but in the end, he failed.

Polyperchon placed a great deal of value on his official standing. He wished to take Alexander's legacy and make it his own; therefore, he attempted to spread his influence in Asia Minor. However, he knew that Antigonus was on Cassander's side, and he couldn't invest in a military campaign to take control of the Asian territory. Instead, he made the decision to bring Eumenes of Cardia into his fold and declare him as the Royal General of Asia. The problem was that Eumenes had been accused and condemned by an official Macedonian council for killing Craterus, meaning Polyperchon had to shamefully offer a special dispensation in order to clear him of the charges. However, restoring his status would be beneficial. Firstly, he wasn't Macedonian; therefore, he could never claim any kind of power, so he would never become a political threat to Polyperchon. Secondly, Antigonus already began his military campaign against him, and with enough support, Eumenes could keep him busy for a long time, away from Macedonia.

Another advantage that Eumenes would bring was of the utmost importance. Antigonus became more and more aggressive in Anatolia, gaining ground rapidly. By that time, he had gained control of the territories east of the Bosporus and Dardanelles. Polyperchon attempted in 317 to stop his advancement by sending a fleet led by Cleitus the White, an admiral who was incredibly successful against the Greeks during the Hellenic War. He won a major battle against Antigonus, but this victory was short-lived. Cleitus would lose most of his fleet during the following night to a carefully planned attacked under the cover of darkness. The admiral was killed, and Polyperchon desperately needed to do something about his rivals.

Eumenes accepted Polyperchon's offer, and with the royal seal in hand, he moved his troops from Cappadocia to go after Antigonus. He began recruiting new troops and taking all the resources he needed from the treasuries he had access to due to his new royal standing. Antigonus was forced to respond to these provocations because he relied on the very same resources in order to gain a foothold in Asia Minor. However, Eumenes was clever enough to push into Iran, where the riches of the old Persian Empire were ready for the taking. He taxed the Iranians and collected enough coin so he could continue to press on to the west. Antigonus had no choice but to pursue his army. He could not allow his enemy to have free access to such wealth.

Eumenes and Antigonus were busy playing a game of cat and mouse in Asia Minor, meaning that Polyperchon was successful in drawing Antigonus' attention away from his actions. However, this wasn't enough. He needed to achieve the same form of victory in Europe as well. What he achieved in Asia Minor wasn't enough to convince the Macedonian courts to join him against Cassander. Polyperchon was painfully aware of this problem, but he quickly formed a plan to build his reputation by allowing Olympias to return to Pella, the capital of Macedonia. This would guarantee him the loyalty of the Argead. At first, Olympias delayed in deciding; however, during the summer of 317, due to Cassander's success in Athens, she chose to accept Polyperchon's offer.

Polyperchon, Alexander IV, and his mother, Roxane, marched under military escort to greet Olympias and bring her to Pella. Arrhidaeus and Eurydice remained behind. This proved to be a fatal error because Eurydice was aware that if Olympias returned, she and her husband would no longer hold all of the power. To avoid this scenario, the two of them contacted Cassander for help. At the same time, Eurydice quickly raised her own army and dispatched them after Polyperchon. The troops obeyed her command until they reached the mountains and were forced to confront the enemy. They immediately surrendered because they couldn't fight against Alexander's own mother and risk igniting a civil war. Eurydice's plan backfired, and it ended solving one of Polyperchon's biggest problems that had been created after Alexander's death: He no longer had to worry about Macedonia being ruled by two kings. Arrhidaeus and Eurydice were apprehended and imprisoned for their traitorous actions against Polyperchon and Olympias. They were treated with great cruelty, and later that year, they were killed.

Polyperchon was right about gaining support by bringing the queen back. However, Olympias' return to Macedonia overshadowed his rule as she began a campaign of revenge against every noble family who had opposed her, especially Cassander's family. Additionally, she ousted more than a hundred Macedonian noblemen who were either against her or who associated with anyone from Antipater's family. Thus began a reign of terror that Polyperchon never expected. As a result, many Macedonians who supported him or who were on neither his nor Cassander's side began to question the rule of law. They started seeing Cassander as a more reasonable option.

In 316, Cassander decided that the time was perfect for his return to Macedonia. The news alone was enough to force Olympias to retreat to Pydna for refuge. However, she acted too late as the roads were blocked by Cassander's men. After a siege, she had no choice but to surrender to him. She was placed under trial, condemned to death, and immediately executed. Alexander IV and Roxane were also captured; however, they were spared. They were both sent to Amphipolis, where they were allowed to live out their lives under close supervision in order to remove the possibility of any rebellious actions.

Cassander benefited from the terror that Olympias unleashed throughout Macedonia. The people were willing to support him as long as he would rule peacefully. This pushed him to further solidify his position by taking Thessalonike as his bride. She was a daughter of Philip II but not Olympias. This gave him even more support as he became a member of the well-respected royal family, that of the great kings Philip and Alexander.

Cassander soon began a campaign for the unhinged support of his people. One of his most remarkable actions was that of raising a new city on the old site of a Corinthian colony that King Philip II conquered in 356. Macedonian settlers would flock to the new urban center and gain the new lands that were distributed to them. Cassander named the new city Kassandreia. He knew that it was an old tradition of Philip's to name every city after himself, which Alexander the Great followed as well. Naming the city after himself helped show the Macedonians that he was the rightful heir and the only equal of the great rulers who had come before. Cassander didn't stop here. He continued urbanization projects in several regions and united scattered communities into an urban center. This type of regional consolidation was started by Philip and Alexander, and Cassander turned it into a Macedonian symbol that would define the Hellenistic period.

Cassander's resounding success forced Polyperchon to retreat to the south with his son. He no longer had any power, influence, or claim to the royal throne because of his support of Olympias' tyranny. However, he still hoped to hold onto the southern territories that Eumenes recovered. Unfortunately, his plans were completely destroyed when he found out that Antigonus had defeated his last supporter. Any political ambitions he had for Asia Minor were gone, and Polyperchon had no choice but to fade away. The only political reaction that mattered belonged to Antigonus. Continuing to support Cassander's rule in Macedonia was an important decision that would affect all of Macedonia. If he decided that Cassander was fit for the throne, Antipater's plan for a two-sided government might come to fruition after all.

Chapter 3 – Antigonus

Timeline:

> 1. 315/14: The beginning of the Third War of the Successors
> 2. 312: Battle of Gaza; Seleucus retakes Babylon
> 3. 311: End of the Third War of the Successors; Macedonia splits

After defeating his rival Polyperchon, Antigonus dealt with his old supporters from the Iranian territories, eliminating any possible threat and resistance. In the year 315, he marched into Persia and then Babylon in order to collect all the gold and silver that was gathered in the royal treasuries. He gathered enough coin to support a large army for several years, and he continued to add to that income due to the tribute he continued to receive from the Iranian governors.

Antigonus used this massive amount of wealth to maintain his position as a royal representative of the Asian government. That position was revoked by Polyperchon, but nobody could contest it. Antigonus' actions had a negative impact on the eastern governors, and it would only become more serious as he continued traveling east as he started deposing the governors who fully embraced

Eumenes as the legal authority. However, the largest impact was felt when he entered Babylon, the territory ruled by Seleucus.

Seleucus was against Eumenes and sided with Antigonus; however, that was about to change. At his court, Seleucus had a violent disagreement with Antigonus regarding the authority he tried to command. Antigonus insisted upon seeing the financial accounts, but the ruler of Babylon denied him. However, Seleucus knew that he didn't stand a chance against him, so he amassed a large army, funded by an enormous amount of wealth.

Seleucus fled to Egypt while he still had the chance. There, he painted Antigonus as a plague on the lands, a man hungry for power and wealth. He claimed that Antigonus wished to take control of the entire Macedonian Empire. Antigonus attempted to counter Seleucus' actions and propaganda by sending his own representatives to the Ptolemaic Kingdom, as well as to Cassander and Lysimachus, the governor of Thrace. His words, however, fell on deaf ears. The other governors and rulers already believed the news brought by Seleucus.

While Antigonus was still busy chasing Eumenes, Ptolemy had secured new territories for himself, namely in southern Syria. At the same time, Cassander attacked whatever resistance was left in Cappadocia. Both of them asked Antigonus to relinquish these lands to them. In addition, Cassander claimed Lycia as well. The governor of Thrace supported both Cassander and Antigonus during this conflict. However, when Antigonus took control of the lands around Hellespontine Phrygia, Lysimachus became worried because Antigonus now had control over a number of his trade routes, so he added to the claims by asking for that territory for himself. This alliance also demanded a part of the riches that Antigonus had amassed after beating Eumenes in battle. They argued that they all contributed to the war; therefore, they should all share the spoils of victory. Antigonus refused all of their demands.

In the winter of 315 to 314, war broke out as a result of challenging Antigonus. From the coalition, Lysimachus posed the smallest threat as he was too busy consolidating his power in Thrace. Ptolemy, on the other hand, was much closer to Antigonus, but he was driven out of Syria. Antigonus began a large ship-building campaign to expand his military might and eventually go on a western offensive. Antigonus wanted to diminish Cassander's position among the Europeans; however, he also knew that he would not stand a chance against the Macedonian military. In addition, Antigonus wanted to avoid attacking Macedonia in order to maintain the possibility of obtaining precious metals and troops from them. His only option at the time was to go to Polyperchon for help.

Polyperchon and his son, Alexander, had retreated to the south and maintained their power in a number of cities in the Peloponnese region. Antigonus was forced to set aside any differences he had with the man and seek his aid. He needed their influence in the region as well as the respect they still commanded among the local populations, and Polyperchon desperately needed resources. An alliance was formed out of the necessity to keep Cassander busy. Polyperchon brought another advantage to the table. Before he was forced to retreat, he restored the Greek cities to their former democracies. At the time, he lost the favor of the rich and powerful oligarchy; however, his decision would now prove to be useful. Four years had passed since then, and Cassander had once again given power over the Greek cities to those who profited from Antipater's reforms. Antigonus knew that having Polyperchon on his side would earn him the support of the people who had once been grateful to him for the restoration of democracy.

Antigonus prepared a new policy that he would enforce with the help from Polyperchon and his son. He couldn't expect any support from any of Cassander's troops or from the rich rulers of the Greek cities; therefore, he decided to focus on the interests of the citizens belonging to the lower classes. His new policy was all about encouraging the Greeks with lower social standing to help themselves and grant him their support. He declared to the Greeks that all of their cities should be independent once again, with the right to self-govern. From the Macedonians, he demanded justice for Olympias, who had been executed by Cassander, as well as for Alexander IV and his mother Roxane, who were being held as prisoners. In addition, Antigonus declared himself as Polyperchon's rightful successor, as he already had his full support.

The demands Antigonus made in the name of Olympias could not be reinforced, but he didn't need them to be. He was sure to gain a few allies in Macedonia because of his stance, but more importantly, he needed to guarantee the loyalty of the Macedonian troops that were still following his command. On the other hand, Antigonus' stance on the Greek issue was practical. He would amass a great deal of influence in the Greek city-states, and he was going to reinforce it by sending a fleet to aid his supporters who struggled against Cassander's oligarchs. The first real success he experienced was thanks to Dioscurides, his nephew, who led a fleet to the Greek island of Delos. Dioscurides helped to ensure their independence, and the Greeks allowed Antigonus to form a foothold from which he could liberate the other cities in time. Other Greek cities were freed in Asia Minor as well. Antigonus' campaign for building up the Greeks' self-determination proved to be a powerful weapon. At the same time, Ptolemy gained power and influence in Cyprus, which was a crucial ship-building center.

Antigonus faced a number of complex issues in Greece. There were many factions, each one with its own ambitions. He could not convince them all to join his side with a simple policy. Antigonus' biggest weakness, however, was his reliance on Polyperchon and his son, Alexander. In 313, Cassander managed to come in between Alexander and his father, convincing Alexander to join his side. This could've turned into a massive blow to Antigonus; however, Alexander was assassinated quickly after his betrayal.

In addition, the smaller Greek cities paid the price for the uncertainty of the times. Some of them were occupied by Cassander's garrisons, while others were liberated by Antigonus. The complications didn't stop there. In some cities, the liberation did not go as planned. The troops eliminating some of the garrisons would later rebel and go on a plundering rampage, destroying the city they freed. One such unfortunate city was Aigion.

Such violent events are an example of the negative impact that resulted from Antigonus' policy of liberation. The rich oligarchy continued to do everything in their power to support Cassander because he guaranteed them control over the local governments. The interests of the upper class and the interests of the lower class were at polar opposites. In many Greek cities, this difference had, in the past, always ignited conflicts, power struggles, and at times even civil war. However, the addition of warring Macedonian dynasties aggravated the Greeks' social condition even more.

For the next three years, Antigonus and Cassander continued their conflict. However, no decisive victor was established. They both suffered losses and defeats, but since none of them were decisive, the war continued.

In 312, though, something changed. Seleucus convinced Ptolemy that they had the perfect opportunity to strike Syria now that Antigonus was busy elsewhere. They both agreed and conquered Gaza as well as other cities without much resistance. Later that year, Antigonus was forced to bring reinforcements to Syria himself. Seleucus was still bitter about what happened in Triparadisus almost ten years before, and he never forgot that he was forced away from his position in Babylonia. He was still chasing his ambitions, so Ptolemy granted him a small army of a thousand men to attempt to gain control over Babylonia. These territories were important to Antigonus because they represented the majority of his financial resources. Without them, he could no longer finance his campaign.

Seleucus increased the size of his small army from the garrisons that Antigonus had left behind. Once he reached Babylon, he had no problems taking over as the city welcomed him back to his seat from which he had governed for four years. Only Antigonus' general, Nicanor, attempted to challenge Seleucus; however, Nicanor suffered a disastrous defeat, forcing him to flee. After this, the local Iranian satrapies reinforced Seleucus' position. Antigonus was forced to react because of Babylon's importance. He sent his son, Demetrius, with a large army of twenty thousand troops. When he arrived in Babylon, Seleucus was in Iran. Demetrius left Patrokles, a commander, in charge of the city's defenses, but he decided to abandon the city. However, Patrokles did leave two citadels fully garrisoned. Demetrius was successful in taking control over one of the citadels. At this point, he made one significant mistake that would lower Antigonus' influence in the region even more: He allowed his troops to go on a rampage and plunder the local population.

Seleucus' resounding success forced Antigonus' hand into open negotiations, which put an end to his western campaign. All sides agreed to the peace talks because they had all suffered losses but gained nothing. The years of war didn't change anyone's influence. Ptolemy maintained his power in Egypt and partially over Cyprus. On the Greek mainland, Antigonus gained some minor support due to his liberation campaign, and in Macedonia, Cassander retained all of his power. In addition, Lysimachus continued to govern in Thrace as he was never truly involved in any major conflicts. In other words, the alliance failed to obtain what they initially demanded. Without Seleucus' intervention in the east, the war might have continued for several more years as neither side suffered significant losses in any of their battles. Since no one was losing anything important, this meant that neither side would be willing to give in to anyone's demands. But since Antigonus lost control of Babylonia, peace was signed by both parties in 311, and they all agreed on formally dividing the Macedonian Empire.

Antigonus had no choice but to agree to the situation in Europe so that he could advance on Seleucus. He was forced to officially recognize Cassander's legitimacy over the European part of the old empire, as well as Lysimachus' dominion over Thrace. Antigonus could no longer hold any claim over any of those territories. Furthermore, he accepted Ptolemy's rule over Egypt and Cyprus. Cassander, on the other hand, was obligated to formally accept the limitations of his position and status within Macedonia. The legitimate heir to the throne, Alexander IV, was still alive. He was twelve years old at the time, and even though he was kept away from the public, he was expected to take on his role as king once he came of age. This decision was made to uphold the Macedonian tradition and appease the masses; however, it would prove to be the death of the young king and his mother. Within two years of the signing of the treaty, they were both killed by the garrison commander Glaucias.

The treaty contained another demand that Cassander was forced to accept in order to close this chapter between the various rulers of the Macedonian Empire. The Greek city-states were to become free and autonomous once more. Antigonus convinced Ptolemy and Lysimachus of the importance of liberating the Greeks. He knew that they wouldn't really care about this clause in the treaty because their territories did not include any of the ancient Greek cities. His goal was to weaken Cassander's political position on the Aegean Islands and mainland Greece. Antigonus knew that Cassander wasn't going to immediately withdraw his military from the cities; however, the message wasn't aimed at him. Instead, Antigonus wanted to boost his own influence and power by assuring the Greeks that their interests were important in this treaty and that the Macedonian rulers must consider their position and status. Direct evidence of Antigonus' strategy was discovered in the small city of Scepsis. There a letter was found that explained why he was making peace. Antigonus wrote that he did not achieve all of his goals for the Greeks because the treaty negotiations would have taken far too long to do so. However, he guaranteed them a clause in the treaty which specified their autonomy. In addition, he expressed that he was forced to compromise some of his principles in the name of peace.

He also mentioned that the Greeks would fight to defend their freedom against any threat and that he would defend their interests. This letter was addressed to Antigonus' own subjects; therefore, there may be some exaggeration in it for his own political reasons.

Chapter 4 – The Seleucid Empire

Timeline:

> 310/309: War between Antigonus and Seleucus in Mesopotamia

The years following the treaty between the Macedonian rulers would prove to be the most influential for the development of the Hellenistic world. This defining period would solidify Hellenism until the Roman invasion and occupation.

The division between the territories in Europe, Asia, and Egypt would become permanent and highly resilient to any attempts to make a change. It was certainly not a natural one, even if it may have looked that way. The only reason it took place was that Antigonus had no real alternative to the ongoing war. Nobody was winning, and nobody was losing. Peace was the only option that wouldn't lead to futile conflicts and economic struggles. The following decade after the peace treaty would only serve to solidify the foundations of the Hellenistic world.

Perhaps one of the most important aspects of the treaty was that Seleucus wasn't present. Since Seleucus wasn't present, the other members of his coalition could not afford to betray him; however, they had to eliminate Antigonus' presence in Europe. This meant restricting him to Asia, but the treaty did not specify what they meant by "Asia," meaning that he would be left to sort it out with Seleucus at a later date. To Antigonus, however, he assumed he had full rights over the Iranian satrapies, as well as Babylon.

Seleucus made his own decision to maintain control over the satrapies and Babylon, and he was supported by Ptolemy. His efforts were focused on controlling the resources and wealth from the satrapies in order to finance his defenses against Antigonus' inevitable attack. With such wealth that overshadowed anything Europe or Egypt could produce, he no longer needed his former coalition allies. However, they would remain friends since they had no intersecting interests that needed to be addressed. This can be seen in the fact that although Seleucus wasn't there to help determine the aspects of the treaty, his former allies didn't betray him. They simply took the only advantage they had, which was making sure to restrict Antigonus to Asia while having their own dominions over Europe and Egypt formally recognized.

Antigonus' biggest challenge was facing Seleucus as soon as possible because he couldn't allow for him to continue controlling the rich satrapies. He needed them for himself in order to maintain his mercenary army. This forced him to march for Babylonia. Historical records of this campaign are vague, and very little is known about it. A part of the Babylonian Chronicles mentions battles taking place in Babylonia in 310 and 309; however, neither of them led to a decisive resolution. What the evidence does show is that Antigonus suffered a major defeat at the end of 309 when he was forced to withdraw to Syria. Historians don't know whether he came to an agreement with Seleucus or whether Antigonus simply no longer had the resources to continue his campaign against him.

Seleucus secured his position in Babylonia and spent the next few years solidifying his rule over the Iranian satrapies. His territories expanded to the Indian border. In 305, he marched across that border to display his military strength to the regional rulers. This campaign would prove to be a disaster. Seleucus was forced to sign a treaty, the Treaty of the Indus, with Chandragupta Maurya, the founder of the Maurya Empire. As a result of the treaty, the Maurya Empire annexed large swathes of the eastern provinces of Seleucus' territories. On the other hand, Chandragupta married Seleucus' daughter, thus forming a marriage alliance, and gave 500 war elephants to Seleucus as well. These war elephants would soon become the core of Seleucus' army.

In a few years, Seleucus would develop his new imperial capital, Seleucia. It was a new city, close to Babylon, which was populated largely by Syrians and Greeks; the Greeks, for the most part, came from his Greek mercenaries and Macedonian soldiers. He maintained the same traditional systems of government in the Iranian satrapies as well as in Babylonia; however, alongside them, he had a Greek administration. He combined the Aramaic aristocracy with the Greek aristocracy, with him in the center. Maintaining such a complex dual-governing system was difficult, and it required Seleucus' personal attention. However, he was successful and created a massive financial monopoly in the region by taking advantage of the abundance of Iranian and Babylonian resources. His new governing system, however, did not change his focus. Seleucus, as well as his future heirs, were still Macedonian at heart, and therefore, they were still interested in what was happening in Greece and Macedonia.

As a result of creating a new, unique Macedonian Empire, Seleucus introduced a new kind of calendar to put an emphasis on the dualistic nature of his government. This included a method of counting time, as well as dating official documents. The Seleucid era had two different starting points. One was meant for the Greek populations, and it was year 312, which was when he conquered Babylon according to the Macedonian calendar. The other was based on the Babylonian calendar, and it was year 311, which was when he ruled Babylon. With this new "era," Seleucus promoted to his subjects a new empire that maintained their old traditions and values. He wanted to make them understand that he did not intend to destroy their way of life.

Between the signing of the treaty in 305 and the year 301, Seleucus would develop a new empire. He became a powerful ruler that would rival any of his former coalition allies.

Chapter 5 – Cassander of Macedonia

Timeline:

1. 310/309: Cassander assassinates Alexander IV and his mother, Roxane
2. 309: Cassander meets Polyperchon in Upper Macedonia
3. 307: Demetrius takes Athens from Cassander
4. 305: Demetrius attacks Rhodes
5. 304: Treaty is signed; Demetrius leaves Rhodes
6. 301: Battle of Ipsus

After the signing of the treaty, the situation in Macedonia was a great deal more complex than in Asia. Cassander was essentially bound to "babysit" the young king until he would reach maturity and officially take his throne. However, he could not let that happen.

The Greek historian and general Hieronymus of Cardia took note of Antigonus' reaction to Cassander's order to assassinate the young king and his mother. He, as well as Ptolemy and Lysimachus, were relieved by his death. There would no longer be any challenge for the throne of Macedonia from the Argead dynasty. This meant that Cassander, Antigonus, and the other Macedonian rulers were officially free to govern their own territories and continue with their personal aspirations. They no longer had to worry about a future king who would seek to claim what was rightfully his.

The assassination in 310/309 marked a new era. Everyone knew the situation, but the old generals waited for several years until they claimed their official titles as rulers. Antigonus was the first in 306. Cassander was especially cautious because the resistance was greater in Macedonia, where many influential people remained loyal to the Argead royal house, even after the cruel governing period under Olympias. This was why Cassander married Thessalonike and why he promoted his connection to Philip instead of to Alexander the Great. Cassander maintained his position in Macedonia without much conflict. However, the situation was different in the Greek city-states.

Cassander maintained control over Athens, but other cities represented a danger to him. Peloponnese was under Polyperchon's control, who still maintained his alliance with Antigonus. The cities of Sicyon and Corinth were ruled by the widow of Alexander, Polyperchon's son. In the west, the Aetolian League still dominated part of Greece as they were never defeated. The Aetolians were entirely independent and against Cassander. Independently, these small territories weren't a significant threat; however, they all shared one common enemy: the new ruler of Macedonia.

Cassander's position was, to some degree, unstable, but he was capable of managing the situation as long as Antigonus remained occupied with Seleucus. Polyperchon was the first to challenge Cassander after the assassination of the last of the Argead royal house. Polyperchon, having served for years under Alexander the Great's command, knew that he had fathered another son with Barsine, an Iranian princess. His name was Heracles, and he was still alive and well at the age of seventeen, living in Pergamon[1]. Polyperchon hoped to regain some of his former status and influence in Macedonia by bringing the last survivor of the Argead house to take his rightful throne. In 309, he escorted Heracles to Upper Macedonia where he met Cassander and his army. Neither of them wanted to risk everything on the battlefield, and Cassander didn't want to see another contender to the throne. He and Polyperchon met face to face, and they made a deal. Heracles was to be eliminated, and in exchange, Polyperchon would receive control over his former estates and become the representative of the southern Greek territories.

Cassander achieved two goals from this encounter. He eliminated another threat to his rule, and he deprived Antigonus of one of his allies. His position in Macedonia was more secure than ever before; however, he still lacked enough influence over the Greek cities. Polyperchon gained what he desired as well since he secured his family's position and titles once more. Cassander even handed him his own troops because he knew he would no longer be a threat to him as Polyperchon was around eighty years old at the time.

In 307, Cassander suffered his first significant loss. Antigonus' retreat from his failed campaign against Seleucus did not put an end to his ambitions. In fact, his position was a strong one. Antigonus didn't challenge Cassander directly, however. He remained in Syria where he was building his new capital and instead dispatched Demetrius with a large fleet. His fleet caused significant losses in Cyprus; however, the large blow came unexpectedly when he attacked and captured the city of Athens. The capture itself was, in fact, purely accidental. It happened because the city's authorities thought they were looking at Ptolemy's fleet; therefore, they didn't raise any defenses. As a result, Athens would remain under

---

[1] It is not known for certain if Alexander the Great actually fathered Heracles. Several sources mention him, but not all do. What is known is that a boy who resembled Alexander was produced by Polyperchon to be used as a pawn during these succession wars.

Demetrius' control over the next two decades. Demetrius allowed the former governor to leave the city honorably, and in the upcoming weeks, he began expelling the Macedonian garrison, as well as the Ptolemaic garrisons, from neighboring territories. This was a significant defeat for Cassander. His position in Greece was already weak, and now, he lost the most important position he held in that region.

Losing Athens to Antigonus was a major blow. Because of the autocratic governing style of Cassander's governor, Demetrius did not encounter much resistance. He continued promoting his father's propaganda of freedom and democracy for all the Greeks. He guaranteed the Athenians that there would be no military garrison holding a sword at their throats. Soon after the city's liberation, the Greeks could once again hold a citizen's council. At the formal assembly, they enthusiastically voted to be represented by Antigonus and his son, Demetrius. In fact, they were so eager to welcome the change that they gave the two rulers the status of saviors. Demetrius' treatment of democratic Athens would be recorded on the many stones, statues, and monuments erected in his name.

Cassander's choice to rule Athens with an iron fist, crushing the democracy and freedoms of the people, proved to be a mistake of which Antigonus took full advantage. Demetrius, on the other hand, chose to follow his father's footsteps. He placed his political focus on winning the Greek citizens to his side by gaining their love and appreciation instead of oppressing them. He followed the terms of the peace treaty that Antigonus signed in 311 and made sure to respect the promises he made to the Greeks, which were the rights to freedom and self-determination. Gaining their love and trust proved to be much cheaper than what it took for Cassander to manage his control over the city.

In the following four years, Cassander would attempt to regain the city; however, the population was determined to keep their freedom and opposed him openly, even when Demetrius was pursuing other objectives. In addition, their capability to resist was amplified by the

Aetolian League, who had helped the Athenians during the Hellenic War. In 304, Demetrius returned to Athens, where he remained for two years. During this time, tensions between himself and the population began to show. The Athenians realized that their freedom extended as far as their new ruler allowed. In other words, they were free as long as they did what he wanted. Demetrius became increasingly authoritarian during that period, moving his residence to the Parthenon and taking more resources for himself and his entourage. However, the Athenians required his presence in order to defend themselves against Cassander's attacks.

Antigonus was skeptical about Demetrius' takeover of Athens and was perhaps just as troubled by it as Cassander was, as Antigonus' priority at the time wasn't Greece. He had dispatched his son's large fleet to gain naval supremacy in the Mediterranean and to push Ptolemy back. Taking control of Cyprus was more important at the time than Athens, so Antigonus recalled Demetrius to send him back to Cyprus.

Demetrius' operations lasted two years until he successfully managed to take over Cyprus. The naval victory represented Antigonus' only true priority in the region, as his main enemy at the time wasn't Cassander but Ptolemy. In 305, Antigonus proved this by sending Demetrius to attack Rhodes, which was an independent republic. The reason for the attack was their refusal to aid Antigonus in his battles against Ptolemy. At the same time, Athens had to defend itself against Cassander's attacks. This new campaign against the island republic lasted a year. It was a pointless siege that demanded a lot of resources and time because Demetrius could not apply the same tactics as he had in Athens. This was already an independent republic, and Demetrius only attacked it because they democratically chose not to interfere in the war against Ptolemy. This siege was one of the reasons why the Athenians began to questions Demetrius' government and his stance on democracy and Greek independence.

The siege on Rhodes was an important event that greatly impacted Antigonus' entire campaign. It was a sign to the other rulers that they could effectively resist him. Cassander, Ptolemy, and Lysimachus helped the inhabitants of Rhodes in different ways in order to ensure that they kept Demetrius busy long enough for him to lose more men and resources. In addition, his Greek allies were becoming increasingly irritated by his persistence in besieging an island that seemingly could not be conquered while they were being attacked by Cassander. Athens attempted to convince Demetrius to drop the siege, but it was the Aetolians who finally managed to convince him to negotiate with the citizens of Rhodes. In 304, they signed an agreement; he lifted the siege and returned to Athens.

The Athenians and Aetolians were willing to forgive Demetrius' senseless persistence on the island of Rhodes, considering it to be a regrettable mistake. They weren't really left with another choice, since Cassander was still powerful in the region and Demetrius was the only ally they had. They obtained what they wished for as Antigonus gave his son permission to begin his operations in Greece and fight against both Cassander and Polyperchon.

Demetrius' campaign in Greece was a successful one. Within two years, he had liberated such a large number of cities that he had to organize them into a sort of federation, taking his inspiration from the League of Corinth, which Philip II created before his war against the Persians. With an alliance of Greek city-states by his side, Demetrius was able to attack Cassander more aggressively. He expanded rapidly into his territory until he received word from his father in 301. The alliance between Cassander, Ptolemy, and Lysimachus had achieved great results during the siege of Rhodes, and now, they were about to work together once more.

Concerned by Demetrius' progress in Greece, they decided to attack Antigonus in his own territories in Asia Minor. However, their greatest asset was, in fact, Seleucus. He joined them in their campaign against Antigonus with his Iranian army and a number of war elephants, but, he did not take the same route as them. Seleucus headed for Cappadocia while the others traversed Asia Minor. The two armies reached Antigonus in Ipsus, Phrygia.

The Battle of Ipsus in 301 BCE marked another stage in the Hellenistic age. The result was the death of Antigonus and the total defeat of his army. This event would later affect the social and political structures within the old Macedonian territories.

Chapter 6 – After the Battle

Timeline:

1. 300: Famine in Athens; Lachares becomes new representative of Athens
2. 297: Death of Cassander
3. 295: Demetrius regains Athens
4. 286: Demetrius goes to Asia Minor
5. 283: Death of Demetrius

The next two decades after the Battle of Ipsus lack historical records. The dates of the following events are uncertain and mostly hypothesized from the many fragmentary documents written by a number of ancient historians. In addition, close to nothing is known about what happened in Egypt and other areas outside of the Hellenistic world.

After Antigonus' death, the victors divided his lands and wealth. Seleucus gained control over Syria, Lysimachus took a number of territories in Asia Minor, and Cassander held dominion over European Greece (except for Thrace). In addition, Ptolemy occupied a part of Lebanon, even though he was not present during the battle.

Other than some newfound tension caused by disagreements between the borders of the Ptolemaic Kingdom and the Seleucid

Empire, the alliance was relatively pleased with the territorial divisions, and they were looking forward to heading their separate ways. They were convinced that the threat was over because Antigonus was dead and his army completely defeated. However, it was a mistake to have made such an assumption. Demetrius was still alive, and he still had full control over his fleet. In addition, he already held the title of king as part of one of his father's precautionary measures. Antigonus was old and had many enemies. Therefore, when he named himself king over his territories, he offered the same title to his son to avoid the same situation the empire faced when Alexander the Great died. This meant that from the Battle of Ipsus, a king rose with a fleet at his back but with no country to rule. However, his naval power was enough to grant him sufficient political significance.

Demetrius maintained control over the harbor city of Ephesus, the island of Cyprus, the Peloponnese, and many of the islands of the Aegean. In addition to his fleet, he relied on one other weapon: the memory of his accomplishments in Athens and other Greek cities that were freed under his rule. This included the federation of city-states he had created during his campaign in Greece. After Ipsus, Demetrius sailed for Athens. During this time, the Athenians heard about the decisive defeat Antigonus and his son had suffered. They took advantage of this to hold a council and agreed to forbid any king from entering the harbor city. Officially, this decision was meant to be a neutral stance and nothing more. However, in reality, it meant abandoning Demetrius. When he arrived at Athens, he wasn't allowed to enter, but he was offered a number of ships that he had left behind before heading to battle. Demetrius decided to gather his entire navy and sail north.

Demetrius intended to attack Lysimachus, but Seleucus drew his attention by offering him an alliance. Seleucus wanted to marry Demetrius' daughter, Stratonice, and seal a marriage alliance that would forever eliminate him as a personal threat. The marriage was a practical decision from both sides as the largest military land force would become united with the largest navy in the Hellenistic world.

In the meantime, the Athenians learned that staying neutral was difficult. The city-state was historically dependent on importing food from other territories, such as Egypt and what is nowadays Ukraine. Both of these regions were controlled by different kings, resulting in famine by the year 300. During this difficult period, the military took over the governing structure of the city, and with Cassander's interference, their control of the city would be maintained. Democracy only survived on the surface as it had no actual importance in any function of the state. Lachares, an influential Athenian politician, became the new representative of the Athenian government.

The next three years were relatively quiet until Cassander's sudden death in 297. In addition, his son, Philip IV, who was supposed to be his heir, died several months later. This new power vacuum had to be filled. Cassander's wife, Thessalonike, acted as a regent for a short period in order to manage her other two sons, Alexander V and Antipater II. However, Antipater II murdered his own mother, removing Thessalonike from the picture, and he began a civil war against his younger brother. Neither of them was experienced in warfare or politics; therefore, they allowed any outside help to come to Macedonia and join a side.

The exact dates during these events are unknown. However, it is known that by 295, Demetrius managed to regain control of Athens. This time, though, liberation and democracy were no longer part of his intentions. He placed people he could trust in every single key position within the Athenian government. Demetrius needed Athens to become the center of his power so that he could push his influence in Macedonia where the civil war between the two brothers continued.

Antipater II requested aid from Lysimachus, while Alexander V sought help from Demetrius and Pyrrhus (the second cousin of

Alexander the Great). Pyrrhus was a valuable ally during the Battle of Ipsus, where he fought alongside Demetrius and Antigonus. He was able to respond to Alexander V' plea much faster than Demetrius and agreed to send him aid. When Demetrius arrived in Macedonia, the war was over. Alexander had won because of the help he received from Pyrrhus. However, he still accepted to see Demetrius. This action was a naïve one because Demetrius took the opportunity to have him assassinated. The boy's own council could not react because they were in the middle of Demetrius' camp. Their only option was to accept Demetrius as the new king. This change in regional politics was embraced by Lysimachus as well, as he had no other choice. He required stability in the area while he was pursuing his own interests along the Danube River. Demetrius had finally reached the goal his father strived for and became the king of Macedonia in 294 BCE.

Even though Demetrius became the king, a goal his father wished to achieve, he only remained in that position for a short period of time. After gaining the throne, Demetrius decided to gather his navy and army to begin his new campaign, as he was eager to march back to Asia Minor. He instructed his son Antigonus II Gonatas to stay in Corinth and maintain order in his place.

His father's old territories had changed since 295 when Demetrius had left for Greece. On his return, he was expecting a welcoming reception from the people; however, he did not receive one. After the Battle of Ipsus, control over Antigonus' lands went partially to Lysimachus. However, he did not have the resources to stabilize his position and guarantee order in all corners of the land. Local tyrants rose up in some of the cities as a result. The power vacuum had to be filled, and Lysimachus, whether he approved of them or not, could not do much to remove the local autocrats. His only choice was to find a way to cooperate with them instead, and he did. There were some exceptions, like in Bithynia, for example, where the local ruler was strong and confident enough to refuse any agreements with

Lysimachus and instead ruled independently in the region. Later on, the new Kingdom of Bithynia would rise from this resistance.

In the Troad region, where Antigonus had been overseeing the construction of his new city Antigonia, Lysimachus took over the project. He continued investing in the new urban development; however, he renamed it Alexandria. Other cities were also fortified and improved. Lysimachus changed the administrative system by grouping a number of cities under a regional administration led by a general. These improvements were made to secure his position and prepare his defenses in case of invasion.

In 286, Demetrius arrived in Miletus, located on the western coast of Asia Minor, anxious to fight. However, he was about to attack a region that had enjoyed roughly fifteen years' worth of development and well-organized administration. Most of the cities were controlled by the local population, and Lysimachus was somewhat popular, though not loved. Demetrius' image as a liberator had no effect over them, and in many cities, he wasn't even welcome. However, being Antigonus' son still carried some weight in certain areas. A number of cities joined his side, but not as many as he would have liked. Demetrius instead brought much of the region to its knees by force.

Many of Lysimachus' soldiers and officers joined Demetrius because they weren't willing to fight him. However, as soon as he was forced to face Agathocles (the son of Lysimachus) on the battlefield, Demetrius retreated and lost most of what he gained during his short campaign in Asia. Demetrius marched for Iran, seeking the aid of the local leaders who had supported his father in the past. It was a desperate move that demonstrated he wasn't a skilled conqueror like Seleucus. Demetrius would learn that building an empire wasn't only about forging alliances and conquering new lands. Ruling an empire required the daily administration of a complex system. His lack of skill was the fatal flaw that prevented him from succeeding in Macedonia, as well as in Asia Minor.

Demetrius did not manage to gain the help he sought. He spent a difficult winter in Anatolia, after which he was captured by Seleucus and taken to Syria in 286. There he would meet his end, but not by the sword. Seleucus allowed him to live his life with some freedom and certain luxuries befitting his standing. In 283, Demetrius would die from excessive drinking.

Chapter 7 – The End of an Era

Timeline:

> 1. 285: Lysimachus becomes king in Macedonia
> 2. 283/2: Assassination of Agathocles by Lysimachus
> 3. 281: Battle of Corupedium between Lysimachus and Seleucus; Lysimachus dies

While Demetrius was occupied with his new campaign in Asia, his son Antigonus II Gonatas was charged with holding several positions in Macedonia, as well as part of Greece, including Corinth and Demetrias. At the same time, Lysimachus took control of eastern Macedonia while Pyrrhus took the western territories. However, Pyrrhus' dominion wouldn't last long as Lysimachus drove him out in a short period of time. Pyrrhus continued his attempts to capture a number of Demetrius' strategic positions in Greece, but he was not successful. He was forced to retreat to his territories in western Greece, which were his by right and supported by the Aetolians.

Lysimachus carved himself a new empire that included Thrace, Macedonia, and most of Asia Minor. His power and influence became greater than Ptolemy's, and he was even rivaling Seleucus at this point. However, the empire wasn't as solidified as he preferred. The main reasons he was able to keep it together were the wealthy nobility who supported his endeavors, the local rulers who controlled many of the cities in Asia Minor, and the loyalty of the military.

Lysimachus was an old man during the height of his empire, and he knew he needed to train his successor. The elite, the imperial administration, and the army all had to support his choice in order to maintain the integrity of the empire. Seleucus, on the other hand, solved his own succession problems. He never joined Antipater's family as other rulers had. Instead, he had married an Iranian wife named Apama and had a son with her around 324 or 323 BCE. So, by the year 290, Seleucus already had a mature son, Antiochus, who was accepted by the local populations. In addition, he named him "king," and they ruled together.

As for Ptolemy, he wasn't as lucky as Seleucus. He was a part of Antipater's family, having married his daughter, Eurydice, and he had fathered several sons and daughters with her. In addition, he took a new wife and begot at least three more children with her. He had many successors that he planned to use in order to establish alliances with the other rulers, the same way Antipater did. The problem was that having several sons from two different wives would inevitably lead to rivalry. His first wife, Eurydice, left the court with her eldest son to avoid any plots from Berenice I, Ptolemy's second wife. They settled in Miletus, far away from Egypt. In 285, Ptolemy declared his son Ptolemy Philadelphus (who he had with Berenice) to be his successor, and he granted him the royal title. At the same time, Ptolemy brought Lysimachus into his family by offering him his eldest daughter's hand in marriage.

Eurydice entered the same game of binding the rulers to her family by using her own daughters. When Demetrius reached Miletus in 286, ready to begin his Asian campaign, she approached him to offer her daughter Ptolemais. She had already secured a marital alliance with Lysimachus by offering her other daughter to Agathocles. Eurydice was making sure that she would be on the side of the winner, no matter who succeeded in the conflict.

Unfortunately, Demetrius' fate was sealed. After his capture and subsequent death, his wife vanished from the records. However, Eurydice still had Agathocles, but she was already losing her ground to Berenice. Lysimachus was an old man, and Berenice's daughter, Arsinoe II, became a large influence on him. While his son was governing his territories in Asia Minor, she was poisoning his mind with thoughts of betrayal. Arsinoe was slowly convincing Lysimachus that his son was going to betray him and take his place. Agathocles was too far away from his father to be able to defend himself against such absurd accusations. He had nothing to gain from conspiring against his father because he was already ruling the empire by his side and about to inherit it upon his death. Unfortunately, Lysimachus gave into his wife's suggestions. Agathocles was executed in 284; therefore, Eurydice lost the alliance she had developed with that house. These actions were devastating to the empire, which heavily relied on well-established relations between the kings and the local administrations. There was no successor worthy of the elite's loyalty.

After the Battle of Ipsus in 301, Seleucus had continued focusing on developing his own empire by setting up a new administrative system capable of organizing such a vast amount of territory and citizens. He began raising new cities to reinforce his dominion over the land and prove that he was superior to the late Antigonus. His son, Antiochus, was charged to govern over Mesopotamia, as well as the Upper Satrapies, a term used to refer to the Iranian satrapies. The main focus in the Seleucid Empire was on infrastructure.

Since the territories were divided and every ruler focused on his own interests after the Battle of Ipsus, Seleucus agreed to the circumstances, as this allowed him to pursue his own goals without much interference. He was satisfied with Lysimachus as his neighbor as long as he didn't challenge his rule, and Seleucus had no reason to go against Ptolemy. In fact, in 286, they came together to stop Demetrius' ambitions. Ptolemy weakened his naval forces by capturing Cyprus and a number of his harbor cities, and more importantly, he managed to take control of the federation of Greek city-states Demetrius had formed.

The status quo began to change around the year 284, with the death of Agathocles. In addition, in 282, Ptolemy passed away due to his advanced age. Seleucus was surprised by the execution of Agathocles, and he didn't know whether he could trust Ptolemy's heir. All of this chaos brooding in both empires appeared as a new opportunity for Seleucus. For years, he had wanted control of the territories which the other rulers led, and in 282, he could finally act by invading Asia Minor as Lysimachus' empire was vulnerable and ripe for the taking.

Seleucus was an old man in his seventies at this point. He had no time to sit and weigh his options. He would either try to pursue his dream or hesitate and die of old age. There is very little information about his military campaign in Asia Minor, but there are sources that show Seleucus reached Corupedium in 281, where he faced Lysimachus' army. Lysimachus died in battle due to a thrown javelin, according to Memnon of Heraclea, a Greek historian. Lysimachus had no successors to take his throne, and his empire had no reason to follow his wife's lead, especially after the upsetting death of Agathocles. Seleucus was greeted as the victor. There was no other choice.

After the battle, Seleucus began marching toward Macedonia while negotiating with local administrations along his way. The death of Lysimachus was also the death of the king of Macedonia. Seleucus himself was Macedonian as well and the last surviving companion of Alexander the Great. The throne belonged to him, and he went to claim it. His destiny was within his grasp; however, as soon as he stepped on European soil, Seleucus was assassinated. The last of the great generals was dead. This assassin was named Ptolemy Keraunos, Eurydice's son. The old generation of rulers was over, but a new one took their place, as young Ptolemy Keraunos was crowned as king of Macedonia.

Chapter 8 – A New Beginning

Timeline:

1. 279: Celtic attacks on Macedonia and Greece; death of Ptolemy Keraunos
2. 277/6: Antigonus II Gonatas becomes king of Macedonia
3. 267: Chremonidean War starts
4. 262: Athens surrenders; end of Chremonidean War

After the deaths of the Macedonian rulers comes a period of obscurity. There are only fragments of historical documents that describe the next sixty years after the Battle of Corupedium in 281. Most information today is taken from later historians that chronicled the events based on the evidence they had at the time.

After Seleucus' death, Ptolemy Keraunos took control of Lysimachus' European territories. His rule was accepted by the elite and by the local population because he was Antipater's grandson. By tradition, he had every right to claim these lands. At the same time, Seleucus' son Antiochus was still alive and well; however, he was occupied claiming his rights to the Asian territories of the old Seleucid Empire.

Other potential challengers still posed a threat, though. Demetrius' son, Antigonus II Gonatas, already carved his own territory with himself as the king. In addition, Lysimachus' son Ptolemy Epigonos was a potential threat to the throne of Macedonia. Out of these claimants, Antigonus II Gonatas was arguably the most powerful one as he ruled over Corinth, Piraeus, Demetrias, and Chalcis, and he still held onto part of his father's navy. Furthermore, he had a sister, Stratonice, who once was Seleucus' wife but became Antiochus' wife in 294 BCE; therefore, he had a potential ally.

Ptolemy Keraunos, however, was able to deal with these threats as he solidified his position. His father left him a great fleet of ships in the Dardanelles, and he was able to use them to defeat Antigonus II Gonatas and to negotiate with Antiochus. Soon after, he dealt with Ptolemy Epigonos as well. Ptolemy Keraunos' most important achievement, though, was securing a friendly relationship with Pyrrhus in exchange for a number of troops and war elephants. Pyrrhus was about to depart for Italy where he would conduct a five-year campaign against the Romans, who, at the time, were a fairly small federation of Italian city-states. Ptolemy Keraunos' position in Macedonia was solid, as all of the challengers were either defeated or busy elsewhere.

Not long after securing his territory, Ptolemy Keraunos was about to face his first real threat. Gallic invaders were swarming into the Balkans and Asia Minor. One faction was pushing into Thrace, while another two were invading Macedonia and Greece via different routes. They were attracted by the massive amount of wealth and resources gathered in Macedonia and the territories in Asia Minor. Ptolemy Keraunos encountered one of the factions led by a man named Bolgios. Unfortunately for Ptolemy Keraunos, his military force wasn't prepared to go against the Gauls as they were still recovering from other battles. In addition, he made the mistake of giving a part of his troops to Pyrrhus. This conflict resulted in his total defeat and death. Macedonia was in chaos, and very little defense could be prepared in time. A new army was quickly assembled, but Gallic reinforcements arrived. Two groups led by

Brennus and Acichorius marched through Macedonia in 279, heading for the Greek cities.

There's a small gap in the story about the Gallic invasion, but it does continue with the brave resistance of a number of Greek city-states against Brennus. Antigonus II Gonatas and Antiochus were present in the conflict, aiding the Greeks by financing a number of mercenary soldiers. The two rulers formed an alliance, hoping to repel the invaders and earn some prestige. Some historical accounts of the period show that they were up against an invading force of 20,000; however, there is no evidence that shows the Macedonians being outnumbered. The Gauls did have an intimidating effect on the Hellenistic armies, though, due to their fierce fighting style and frightening appearance.

Encountering heavy resistance, the Gauls changed their strategy and shifted part of their attention toward the Aetolian League. A massacre took place in the city of Kallion where the Aetolians were completely unprepared. However, the Gauls underestimated the defenders. The level of cruel destruction the Gauls left behind angered the mountain folk. They waged a guerrilla campaign in the mountains, picking away at the Gallic army. Even the Aetolian women participated in these skirmishes. The Gauls suffered many losses on that front. In the meantime, Brennus and Acichorius marched to Delphi with the plan to plunder the shrine of Apollo. The Aetolians continued harassing the invaders until the early winter weather took its toll on the Gauls. It was autumn when premature snow and winter storms manifested themselves. These acts of nature emboldened the Greeks and the Macedonians. They believed that Apollo himself came to aid them in the battles. During the defense of Delphi, Brennus was injured, and the Gauls were forced to retreat. Brennus eventually died from his wounds, and the rest of his troops headed north, giving up on any dreams of plunder.

Most of the Gauls retreated to the Danube, where they formed the Kingdom of Tylis. From there, they continued raiding the Greek coasts. A number of them remained in Greece and Macedonia, where they joined mercenary armies belonging to the wealthy elite. One group, however, marched into Asia Minor where they briefly battled Antigonus II Gonatas before dissolving into mercenary armies as well.

Shortly after the defeat of the Gauls, the Aetolian League began expanding in central Greece because there was no one who could oppose them. Antigonus II Gonatas, who was officially the king of Macedonia at this time, was busy solidifying his position, and he seemingly ignored the new expansion. He preferred to maintain friendly relations with the Aetolian League in the next several years. During this time, he bolstered his naval capabilities with help from Antiochus. His rise as a naval power reminded the people of his father, Demetrius. The house of Ptolemy saw this as a potential threat, and Ptolemy II Philadelphus was increasingly worried.

Officially, Ptolemy II Philadelphus was married to his sister, Arsinoe II, who had been previously married to two Macedonian kings, namely Ptolemy Keraunos and Lysimachus. Arsinoe still held onto her ambitions in Macedonia. Some historians think that she might have been the reason why Ptolemy II Philadelphus developed a hatred for Antigonus II Gonatas. This animosity was reflected in his policies. Using his wife's influence, Ptolemy II forged an alliance with Athens as well as Sparta, and the elite from the Greek cities started developing a league that would oppose Macedonian rule.

In 268, Chremonides, an Athenian statesman, issued a decree that suggested creating an alliance between Athens, Sparta, and Ptolemy II. He stimulated the Greek assembly with the use of patriotism, giving an example of how Sparta and Athens faced Persia together over two centuries before. They had once united to preserve their independence while facing a powerful adversary, and they could do so again. Chremonides also claimed that they were facing the same situation that could lead to the loss of Athenian liberty. The famous Decree of Chremonides did not mention who the common enemy was supposed to be. However, he did compare this enemy to Xerxes, and the only man threatening enough at the time was Antigonus II

Gonatas, the king of Macedonia. Antigonus II wasn't liked by the Greeks because he applied the same methods of control as Xerxes. The Greek cities under his rule were secured and controlled by his military garrisons, and their freedoms and right to assembly were taken away.

The Decree of Chremonides, from which a new alliance was born, soon led to a new war, nicknamed the Chremonidean War.

Antigonus II held significant power when it came to land battles. Corinth was one of the main cities that was prohibiting the advancement of the Greeks and their new alliance. In addition, his own Greek territories were well connected to Macedonia due to his friendly pact with the Aetolians. On the other hand, Ptolemy's main power was his navy. His garrisons were scattered on a number of islands, and it would have been difficult for him to assemble a significant land force, even when accounting for the Athenians. Antigonus II had the advantage of a better land infrastructure and a larger number of military bases close to each other. Nonetheless, in 267, a battle ensued, starting with the fortress at Rhamnous.

A series of battles and naval blockades followed in the next five years. The coalition took advantage of their superior navy, but it proved to not be enough due to Antigonus II's advantage on land. Naval blockades proved to be nearly useless because the Macedonian garrisons could simply hold out until they received reinforcements by land. By 261, after many battles, heavy losses for the alliance, and a lack of progress, Athens surrendered. The entire campaign was a logistical nightmare from which they didn't gain anything. Chremonides left the city and retreated to Alexandria. The coalition lost, and as a result, Athens was once again under the control of a Macedonian military garrison. The city would remain under Macedonian dominance for the next three decades. A number of Greek fortresses were also taken by Antigonus II. The coalition's failed attempt at eliminating the Macedonian threat had the opposite effect of what the Greeks wanted. Thanks to Chremonides' efforts to start this war, Antigonus II captured new cities in Greece and solidified Macedonian control within the region once again.

Chapter 9 – Europe after the Chremonidean War

Timeline:

> 1. 239: Death of Antigonus II Gonatas; Demetrius II inherits the throne
> 2. 235: Megalopolis joins Achaean League; Cleomenes III becomes new king of Sparta
> 3. 229: Death of Demetrius

This part of Hellenistic history is shrouded in mystery as very little information survived. What is known is that in the following years, Macedonia solidified its position of power in the Hellenistic world. The Achaean League of Greek city-states in Peloponnese developed into a reputable force and remained defiant to the Macedonian king. Sparta retreated from its former position of power as a result of the failed campaign against Antigonus II.

The Aetolian League expanded at a steady rate without any military conflicts. However, piracy became a serious problem in the region. In order to improve their standing, the Aetolians began extending their protection to other states that maintained friendly relations with them. In the following twenty years, the two Greek coalitions of states became significant powers in regional politics. They created an alliance of sorts that rivaled Macedonia itself.

Antigonus II may have solidified his power with the addition of Macedonian garrisons in each city and by instating local tyrants, but he still could not control most of Greece. In addition, Ptolemy II Philadelphus (and later Ptolemy III Euergetes) supported the Achaean League by offering them significant financial resources to boost their military and expand their territories.

The prolonged funding resulting from Ptolemy II's policies led to a new Achaean expansion. One of the most notable actions was the elimination of the garrison in Corinth. The city had been successful against the coalition of Athenians, Spartans, and Ptolemy II Philadelphus in the past; however, through a successful covert operation, the Achaean League took control of it. Other cities soon followed.

One of the largest changes in the Hellenistic political landscape of the time occurred in 239 when Antigonus II died at the age of eighty. His son, Demetrius II, inherited the throne under the guidance of his mother-in-law, Olympias II of Epirus, and Macedonian interests and policies began to shift as a result. Olympias didn't trust the Aetolians, and soon after Demetrius' coronation, a new war began.

Nicknamed the Demetrian War, Demetrius' actions caused the two Greek leagues to form an alliance of convenience. Their cooperation was successful as both of them began expanding farther by capturing a number of Macedonian cities and fortresses. One of the largest victories was obtaining the city of Megalopolis without a fight. Lydiadas ruled Megalopolis as a tyrant, but he was a supporter of Macedonian interests. However, in 235, he found himself isolated from the rest of the kingdom, and so, he decided to join the Achaean League. This maneuver proved to be beneficial as he obtained a powerful position in the coalition. The inhabitants didn't object as they had grown increasingly worried about their Spartan neighbors who were starting to show new signs of hostility. Megalopolis joined the league in order to obtain a higher degree of protection against their historical enemies, the Spartans.

In 235, Sparta was going through a state of change as a new king rose to power, Cleomenes III. His objective was to turn Sparta into a dominating force on the peninsula. Since the Achaean League continued their expansion by welcoming Megalopolis and a number of other neighboring cities, they became Sparta's focus. The two powers were neighboring each other, and confrontation could not be avoided for long. Both of their leaders desired to assert their own dominance over the Peloponnese.

There is very little information about Demetrius II's actions during that period of strife. What is known, however, is that he wasn't successful against the Aetolian League. At the same time, a tribe of Illyrians known as the Ardiaei started pillaging along the shorelines of the Peloponnese, as well as the inland region of Epirus. Demetrius hoped to take advantage of the situation and use his influence to negotiate peace between the invaders and the citizens of Epirus. He was successful, and he convinced Epirus to accept the Illyrians to help fight against the Aetolians. Under the leadership of Agron, the Illyrians began an aggressive campaign against the Aetolians; however, some of them continued with the raids along the coast.

In 231, Agron died, and his wife, Teuta, took over his former position and continued the agreement her husband made. In 230, she launched a large and aggressive campaign against the Aetolian League. Epirus wasn't spared either as the Illyrians decided to capture their capital city, which was defended by a small number of Celtic mercenaries. The citizens no longer wanted to involve Demetrius, and they sought help from the two leagues instead. Both of them agreed to help the Epirotes by sending their armies to drive the Illyrians out. However, they weren't as successful as they hoped. They suffered a number of losses in ships and troops as they tried to defeat the Illyrian defenses in Corfu.

While the Illyrians were still a threat, Demetrius II continued losing ground in the south. The two leagues proved to be a formidable alliance that became recognized as one of the major powers in the Hellenistic world. They continued taking Macedonian territory, and not all of it by force. Their reputation convinced a number of cities, including some from Thessaly, to abandon Macedonian rule and join them instead.

In 229, the situation in Macedonia degraded even more with the death of Demetrius II. The cause isn't known, but it is assumed to be the result of his war in the north against the Dardanians. Demetrius' son, Philip V, was too young to rule, so his cousin, Antigonus III Doson, was named regent.

The loss of Thessaly was a major blow to Macedonia. The Athenians were now emboldened to expel the Macedonian garrisons, even though they had resisted the two leagues. Diogenes, the commander of the garrison, recognized the weakening of Macedonian power in the region, and he opened discussions with the Athenians. He agreed to retreat from the city with the condition that his troops and the evacuation would be paid for by the citizens. The Athenians managed to raise the necessary funds through personal contributions, and all the Macedonian soldiers were paid to leave Athens, as well as a number of outposts surrounding the city. In addition, Diogenes was granted the status of an Athenian citizen.

After the Athenians liberated themselves once again, the Achaean League hoped to bring the city into its alliance of states, making a contribution to the city's treasury to help sway Athens to join. However, Athens decided to remain neutral. The Athenians had to be careful because they were in a precarious state. If they joined, they risked drawing the Macedonian regent's anger, so they declined forming a collaboration with any of his enemies. On the other hand, other Greek and Macedonian cities made the decision to enter the league willingly. This led to an increased rate of expansion of the two leagues, and Macedonia was forced to turn inward and defend itself.

Chapter 10 – Egypt and the Ptolemaic Dynasty

Timeline:

1. 246: Death of Ptolemy II Philadelphus

Ptolemy II Philadelphus did not participate at the Battle of Corupedium in 281. However, the king of Sidon was present with the support of the Nesiotic League (or League of Islanders) in the Aegean. Ptolemy II had control of this coalition of islands, and after Lysimachus' fall in battle, he used his influence to take control of Samos. In addition, he enforced his authority over Miletus while Antiochus I was occupied organizing his territories after the death of his father.

In the following period, Ptolemy II focused on solidifying his new coastal territories in Asia Minor and developing friendly relations with the islands of Rhodes and Kos. During this time, Ptolemaic rule enjoyed the freedom of expanding without any serious opposition from the Seleucid Empire or other potential challengers. In other words, Egypt was about to experience a golden age under the Ptolemaic dynasty.

In Egypt, Ptolemy II began enforcing the traditions and policies of the former Macedonian rulers by mixing the two cultures. He started temple-building projects throughout the territory, which would later be continued by Ptolemy III. In addition, an educational initiative was started as well. Egypt lacked the institutions that led to the improvement of the Hellenistic quality of life. At first, Ptolemy II's soldiers began funding their own schools in the same European style as back home. Soon after, the administration took notice and took measures to encourage this enterprise. For instance, Ptolemy II eliminated the taxes on salt for Greek teachers, which usually had to be paid by everyone living under his rule. Furthermore, Greek festivals and sports events were encouraged and funded by the elite. Greek athletes and trainers received the same benefits from the government.

New urban centers were developed during this period in Egypt. Ptolemy II brought many Greek immigrants to settle the land. Ptolemais and Alexandria are the most prominent examples of new Greek settlements. Ptolemais became notable for its emphasis on Greek culture and the cult of Dionysus. Greek musicians, actors, poets, and dancers also flocked to the new cultural center. Alexandria, on the other hand, expanded rapidly as the region experienced a massive economic boom. Being a major harbor city attracted a large amount of trade for Egypt. In addition, Ptolemy funded the construction of the famous Pharos of Alexandria, also known as the Lighthouse of Alexandria. This project led to improvements in navigation and the further expansion of the docks and warehouses. In the following years, other institutions, such as an academy of sciences as well as a library, were funded and built. This library would later become the largest in the world, famously known today as the Great Library of Alexandria. The city life was dominated by Greek culture, science, religion, and sports. Ptolemy II's purpose for this city was to attract as many Greek immigrants as possible by offering them something that was very rare in the Hellenistic world. The large city also attracted a number of Jews as well, thus mixing the Greek environment with Egyptian and Jewish influences. Alexandria became a diverse city, which resulted in the Greek translation of the holy texts carried by the members of the Jewish faith.

The Ptolemaic dynasty merged with the Egyptian environment as much as it had with the Greek one. The Egyptians had always valued their pharaoh because he was more than just their political leader and representative; he was a connection to the divine that was crucial to the balance and order in society. This meant that Ptolemy II Philadelphus had to take on this role as well. His office required him to participate and lead a series of religious and cultural ceremonies, and he also had to travel to various temples throughout the year and perform the necessary rituals.

At the same time, a Greek festival was dedicated to the cult of Ptolemy. It was similar to the Olympic Games, and it was organized once every four years. The elite started a political campaign to promote Alexandria's games in the entire Hellenistic world. Ptolemy himself wanted it to be recognized by everyone as a legitimate equivalent to the Olympics. This new endeavor was an expensive one, and the regional leaders within the Ptolemaic Empire recognized the amount of coin such an event would cost them, but being placed under enormous pressure, they all had to accept it. Traditionally, the winners of the competitions were rewarded from each city's treasury, which could involve a lot of resources if many contestants participated. To avoid this issue, the League of Islanders met and agreed to share the costs and fund three representatives that would travel to Alexandria.

Immediately after the death of Lysimachus in 281, Ptolemy II's sister, Arsinoe II, fled from Lysimachus' court to that of her brother Ptolemy Keraunos in Macedonia. Following the murder of her two sons by Ptolemy Keraunos, Arsinoe II fled Macedonia for Egypt sometime between 280 and 273 BCE. He was immediately charmed by her, and he took her as his wife, even though she was his full sister. In doing this, he had to repudiate his first wife, Arsinoe I, exiling her to Coptos in Upper Egypt. In Egypt, marriage between siblings wasn't out of the ordinary; however, the Greeks and Macedonians did question such behavior. While such a marriage was normally forbidden in the Hellenistic world, there would be many more in the Ptolemaic dynasty. Another unusual characteristic of this marriage was that Ptolemy's wife shared stately responsibilities, which was unique in the history of the dynasty. There are many such examples in Macedonian history, but with this move, Ptolemy II had also set a precedent for future queens with enough ambition to rule Egypt on their own.

Some of the Greeks still challenged the matrimony between siblings, but Ptolemy II used it to his advantage. He argued that the divine gods were on their side and that they had only done the same as Zeus and Hera, who were also brother and sister and married to each other. In fact, Ptolemy took an additional step to consecrate himself and his wife by creating the cult of "Sibling-Loving Gods." New rituals, ceremonies, and festivities took place in their name throughout Egypt. Once Arsinoe II died in 270, her cult was promoted by the state throughout the kingdom. Temples were erected in her name, including in Alexandria, and she became a goddess to both the Egyptians and the Greeks.

When Ptolemy II Philadelphus died in 246, the religious cult surrounding his family was well established in the minds and hearts of the Greeks and Egyptians. While other Hellenistic cities had their own cults dedicated to certain heroes like Alexander the Great, they were merely created as a sign of honor and respect. The cult of Ptolemy and Arsinoe II was entirely different. It became a symbol of loyalty and power for the Greek and Egyptian elite.

In later years, the cult was developed further by Ptolemy III. A new decree was signed for a gathering of all priests to take place on his birthday. At these synods, it was decided to spread the cult further by focusing specifically on Ptolemy III and his wife, Berenice II. They were named "Benefactor Gods," and their faces and titles were engraved on numerous tablets which were then placed in every temple. Additionally, the Egyptian priests had to use the title of the Benefactor Gods along with their own (for instance, Priestess of Isis and the Benefactor Gods). Their official status would be used on all documents of the state, as well as holy objects used by the priests. Soon after, the royal couple made sure their cult would never drown in obscurity by weaving it into the calendar. During Ptolemy III's rule, he attempted to reform the Egyptian 365-day calendar by adding a day every four years to represent the solar leap year more accurately. This extra day would honor him and his wife as gods equivalent to the children of Nut. The proposal was resisted by the Egyptian priests and people, and it was abandoned until the establishment of the Alexandrian calendar by Emperor Augustus in 25 BCE.

The royal couple didn't encounter any resistance to developing their cult, mainly because they were benevolent toward the Greek and Egyptian temples. They invested in the old ones and built new ones as well. In addition, they recovered the relics and temple treasures that were taken by the Persians. Ptolemy III returned everything to the temples. Furthermore, the people were on their side due to their actions during one of the greatest famines caused by a low Nile flood. Normally, Egypt produced enough food to feed other kingdoms and empires. However, during the time of famine, Ptolemy immediately started importing grain from Syria, Cyprus, and other Hellenistic territories. The cost of these imports was enormous, but they guaranteed eternal appreciation from the population. Ptolemy used the crisis to show both the priests and the people that he could bring order to chaos, just like the ancient pharaohs. Under his reign, Egypt continued to prosper.

Chapter 11 – Change in Egypt

Timeline:

1. 221: Ptolemy IV Philopator becomes king in Egypt
2. 219: Antiochus III attacks Seleucia by the Sea
3. 217: Peace between Ptolemy IV and Antiochus III

Ptolemy IV Philopator ascended his father's throne around the age of 23 in the year 221, with his father dying the previous year. His succession to the throne didn't go unchallenged. His mother, Berenice II, wanted her younger son, Magas, to rule instead. Some courtiers favored Lysimachus, the brother of the late Ptolemy III. Despite all these various bids for power, there was one man who managed to push Ptolemy IV to succession. His name was Sosibius, an Alexandrian who was favored by the late king. He managed to arrange the deaths of Lysimachus, Magas, and Berenice II in a short amount of time. These acts catapulted Sosibius' influence in the court, and with Ptolemy IV on the throne, no one could challenge him. Agathocles, a personal friend of his, also rose to power and was considered, together with Sosibius, to be the governor of Ptolemaic Egypt.

Ptolemy IV was the first ruler of the Hellenistic age that was considered to be unsuitable, as he preferred private pleasures over the affairs of the state. He had no interest in politics and relied on his ministers to perform all of his public duties. He stabilized the dynasty by marrying his younger sister, Arsinoe III, thus monopolizing all the power. The fact that Ptolemy IV wasn't actively taking part in politics didn't affect Egypt's stability. This was due to the strong policies and administrative bureaucracy of the Egyptian court established by his predecessors. Any unprecedented situation that needed to be dealt with was quickly resolved by Sosibius.

A new war began when the ruler of the Seleucid Empire, Antiochus III, successfully attacked Seleucia by the Sea in 219, which was under Ptolemaic control at the time. Antiochus continued progressing through Ptolemy IV's lands, but he struggled, finding resistance in each city. In the end, he did manage to overtake Tyre, but he was so weakened that he made no attempt on Egypt itself. Fruitless negotiations began and only served the purpose of buying time for Sosibius to recruit more mercenaries and convince Ptolemy IV to show himself to the troops and boost their morale. Ptolemy IV personally led the expedition to retake Tyre. Seeing their pharaoh, the Egyptian troops became so inspired that they won the battle without many losses and secured Ptolemy's hold on Coele-Syria. Sosibius negotiated with Antiochus III and allowed him to keep Seleucia by the Sea.

Sosibius mastered the events during this war, but they were not without repercussions. The internal stability of the Ptolemaic state was suffering. Rebel guerilla troops started their attacks throughout the country and fought against the Ptolemaic regime as well. These guerilla attacks continued after the death of Ptolemy IV, who was the last ruler of the dynasty to rule with ease over his inherited kingdom.

Ptolemy IV was also the last ruler of the Ptolemaic dynasty who played a major role in the politics of the Aegean area. His father, Ptolemy III, had built friendly relations with neighboring states, especially with Athens, once the city had freed itself from Macedonian dominion. Good relations with neighbors allowed Ptolemy IV to maintain his presence and prestige in other Macedonian monarchies. It also prevented the Antigonid and

Seleucid kings from gathering sufficient strength to threaten the interests of Ptolemaic Egypt.

Sosibius and Agathocles had a less aggressive view toward affairs in the Aegean area, unlike Ptolemy III, especially after winning the aforementioned war. Egypt acted as a mediator for peace between friendly Greek states and Antiochus III. In 217, the Rhodians, accompanied by representatives from Ptolemy, managed to convince Philip V to negotiate peace. It is not known why Egypt wanted Philip to make peace, especially because at that time, peace would have negatively impacted Ptolemaic commercial interests in foreign politics. Eight years later, when war between Philip V and the Aetolians raged yet again, Sosibius worked in favor of peace. Philip V's desire to strengthen his influence outside of Macedonia and the sudden death of Ptolemy IV in 204 led to political turmoil in Alexandria. Both these facts influenced the Ptolemaic position in the Aegean basin. Rival Macedonian dynasties, the Antigonids and the Seleucids, ruled by Philip V and Antiochus III, respectively, at this point in time, found common ground and managed to build a strategic cooperation. This marks the beginning of the last phase of the struggle for supremacy in the Macedonian world of the Hellenistic age.

Chapter 12 – Asia

Timeline:

1. 223: Death of Seleucus III
2. 222: Death of Ptolemy III
3. 220: Antiochus wins war against Molon
4. 217: Battle of Raphia
5. 213: Antiochus' army captures Sardis

In 223, Seleucus III was assassinated, having ruled for little over two years. His army tried to persuade his uncle, Achaeus, to take the throne for himself, but he refused in favor of Seleucus' younger brother, Antiochus III. At first, he relied on his ministers and advisors in the matters of politics, especially Achaeus, who was given command of Asia Minor. The command of the Upper Satrapies was given to Molon, who was a general. The king himself settled in the center of his lands, thus being able to devote his attention to all corners of the empire.

The new king had to be married, and a suitable wife was found in Laodice III, the daughter of Mithridates II of the Pontic Empire. It was important to bind the independent Pontic kingdom to the Seleucid rule, and a quick marriage was the most accessible way. After barely a year of marriage, Antiochus III had his first son and potential successor, who was also named Antiochus.

Hermeias was Antiochus' chief minister, and he had great influence over the court. He also yearned to strengthen Seleucid power in Ptolemaic south Syria, known as Coele-Syria; this area now forms part of modern-day Lebanon and Syria. He claimed that if the young king led the campaign himself, he would gain much needed military prestige and would discourage his enemies from challenging him. Coele-Syria was an attractive goal at the time because the Seleucid dynasty had an old claim on it, going back all the way to Seleucus I and his success at Ipsus in 301. In 222, just as Hermeias began military preparations to attack Coele-Syria, Molon proclaimed Media to be independent and even issued coins with his own image and title. Antiochus' council came to a decision to split forces and attack Coele-Syria while going against Molon on a second front. The king was to lead the forces and attack Ptolemy III while his generals would fight in Mesopotamia. However, the sudden death of Ptolemy III in 222 made southern Syria even more attractive, and therefore, Antiochus and Hermeias began their campaign.

Molon managed to defeat the army that was sent against him. He even occupied Mesopotamia, including Seleucia on the Tigris, which was the dynastic capital. The seriousness of Molon's threat became obvious to young Antiochus III. He broke off the invasion of Syria and directed his royal armies toward Mesopotamia. By the spring of 220, Antiochus was victorious, and the war against Molon was over. Molon committed suicide to avoid capture, and his body was crucified. Antiochus won prestige in the war against Molon, and he gained the support of his people. Hermeias, on the other hand, lost his influence and significance in court as he had shown hostility toward the king's plans to personally lead the army to Mesopotamia. This led to his assassination, which was justified by the fact that he was plotting against the king. Antiochus was aware of the plot to assassinate Hermeias and did nothing to stop it. In doing so, he freed himself from the influence of the last member of the old generation of court officials.

Antiochus III didn't abandon the idea of conquering south Syria and Palestine, and he concentrated all his energies to engage in wars for them for the next two years. For the Seleucid dynasty, it was common to divide the rule of the lands. By this tradition, Antiochus may have agreed to leave Asia Minor in charge to his uncle Achaeus, while he would rule over south Syria and Palestine once his war efforts were successful. However, Achaeus' army believed he wanted to attack Antiochus and abandoned him. The fact that Antiochus didn't defend his empire from his usurper uncle leads to the belief that an agreement was made about dividing the rule. But, in the summer of 217, the big Battle of Raphia was a failure, and Antiochus lost, meaning his plans to rule over Ptolemaic Syria and Palestine were gone. So, he proclaimed Achaeus a traitor and returned to Asia Minor to challenge his uncle. All the events surrounding Achaeus at that time seem to point to Antiochus recognizing his uncle as a joint ruler but that he changed his mind after the Syrian efforts collapsed. It is probable that later historians were conditioned to change these events and to write Antiochus' version where Achaeus is portrayed as a rebel and betrayer.

In the meantime, Achaeus had gained popularity, and Antiochus didn't have an easy passage through Asia Minor. Only in 213 did Antiochus' royal army manage to capture the city of Sardis, where Achaeus made his headquarters. Later that year, Achaeus himself was captured and mutilated. His extremities and head were cut off, and his body was impaled. Antiochus III finally ruled unchallenged.

During 210 or 209, Antiochus started including his son in daily politics and even gave him a royal title because Antiochus was preparing an excursion in the easternmost parts of the country to restore Seleucid authority. The rich land of Bactria was his main goal, but this land had enjoyed independence since 245 and would be a challenge. It took two years of besieging the capital to get the leaders to negotiate. Antiochus agreed to recognize Bactria's leader Euthydemus I as a king and formed a formal alliance with him that was sealed by the marriage of Antiochus' daughter with Euthydemus' son, Demetrius. In exchange, Antiochus received war elephants and rations to supply his army. Before heading back home, Antiochus crossed into the Kabul valley, and with a show of force, he renewed his alliance with the local Indian king, Sophagasenus. Afterward, he returned home to Seleucia on the Tigris. From there, he ventured down the Persian Gulf to Gerrha. The Gerrhaens paid a great tribute to Antiochus, and he left with the treasure in hand. The prestige he won in these military expeditions brought him the title Megas (The Great), but he never used it officially when referring to himself.

Chapter 13 – The First Macedonian War

Timeline:

> 1. 221: Death of Antigonus III Doson; Philip V becomes king of Macedonia
> 2. 215: Philip V seeks alliance with Hannibal Barca
> 3. 214: War between Rome and Philip V
> 4. 205: Peace of Phoenice; end of war between Rome and Philip V

The main event of 221 in Europe was the death of the Macedonian king, Antigonus III Doson, and the succession of his cousin, Philip V. Philip was considered too young when he took the crown as he was only seventeen years old. But he was the only choice in order to preserve the monarchy. Philip's advisors for the first few years of his rule were determined by Doson's will, and the events that marked Macedonia of that era revolved around the rivalry between these advisors. Philip fought vigorously to break free from their influence, and the beginning of his rule was bloody and violent as he often plotted against his advisors in the attempt to get rid of them.

Philip V was young and energetic; he wanted to prove himself and show that he could be a real king to Macedonia. He engaged in the battles against the Aetolians, where he helped his allies stop Aetolian expansion and prevent their influence from spreading. The destruction of lands around central Greece was costly, and in the early summer of 217, peace was achieved through a treaty, with all sides retaining what they held at the time.

After the war with Aetolia, Scerdilaidas became one of the most influential Illyrian kings. He provoked Philip V by raiding the Upper Macedonian territory known as Dassaretis. During the winter of 217/216, Philip imported Illyrian shipwrights and built himself a fleet of 100 pirate *lembi* (warships), which were ready to set sail and challenge Scerdilaidas. He expected no reaction from Rome because Rome was occupied with Hannibal Barca's attacks in Etruria at the time. But Scerdilaidas sent a missive with the news of Macedonian interference in Roman territory, and just the mere rumor of the arrival of Roman ships was enough to discourage Philip and make him turn back.

In 215, Philip V approached Hannibal asking for an alliance against Rome. This alliance wasn't yet official, nor did Philip and Hannibal have the chance to cooperate, when Rome intercepted the documents that had yet to be approved by Philip. This was enough for Rome to consider this to be a betrayal that would never be forgotten. Rome responded in 214 by sending a number of ships to Illyrian waters. The war continued for the next nine years. Rome created the image of Philip joining Hannibal as being an aggressive act toward them in order to justify their own actions in the war. Unwillingly, the Achaean League was dragged into the war with Rome. In 214, Philip sent 120 *lembi* to Illyria and was busy with the attack on Apollonia when the Roman fleet arrived. Philip was no match for the Roman battleships, so he decided to set fire on his own and retreat to Macedonia by land. Philip spent the next few years successfully avoiding the Roman fleet and any direct confrontation with its armies. He continued his efforts in Illyria on land, where he was successful, and in 212, he managed to take Scerdilaidas' fortress, Lissons.

In 211, the Roman commander Marcus Valerius Laevinus made a pact with the Aetolian League, who had no love for Philip V. They joined forces and fought against Philip and his allies. The league's allies, Sparta, Elis, Pergamon, and Illyria, all joined the war against Philip. Rome had one goal: to keep Philip V occupied in Greece and separate him from Hannibal in Italy. They had no interest in taking lands, but they also did not want peace. However, the Aetolians had other goals they wished to pursue, and they were unhappy with their Roman allies not helping them to capture Acarnania. They were also growing weary of war, and they wanted to end it. Since Hannibal had left Italy and the Roman forces were needed in the African campaign, Rome agreed to peace. Philip was allowed to keep much of what he managed to take during the wars. However, Parthini and Dimale were exceptions, as these cities were old Roman allies. The peace treaty was signed in the capital city of Epirus, Phoenice, in 205, officially ending the First Macedonian War.

Chapter 14 – The Rise of Rome

Timeline:

1. 204: Death of Ptolemy IV Philopator
2. 199: Coele-Syria and Palestine taken by Antiochus III
3. 196: Antiochus III crosses the Dardanelles
4. 196: Rome declares all Greek cities free

The events that took place after the Peace of Phoenice changed the structure of the Hellenistic world permanently. In 204, Ptolemy IV suddenly died, leaving his five-year-old son, Ptolemy V, as his successor. His advisor Sosibius died around the same time, so the struggle for influence in the Ptolemaic court began. Arsinoe III, the mother of Ptolemy V, was assassinated in 204 before she even heard of her husband's death, and so were his family and associates. Although it was proclaimed that Ptolemy V was the ruler now and that he would continue the regime of his father, it is no wonder Philip V and Antiochus III saw the Ptolemaic lands in the Aegean, Asia Minor, and Syria as a prize worth grabbing.

Philip V sought not to provoke Rome and Aetolia and concentrated his forces on the North Aegean and southwestern Asia Minor. He managed to reorganize the military system and build a fleet. Even though Philip operated mostly in traditional Macedonian areas, such as the Axios valley and in the valley of Hebros, Philip V managed to provoke the Rhodians by sending a small fleet commanded by Heracleides of Tarentum to operate in the Aegean. The Rhodians claimed he was responsible for starting a major fire in their dockyards, although this has never been proven.

After 204, the Seleucid expansion in Asia Minor had been halted. The death of Ptolemy IV offered Antiochus III a new opportunity to reclaim Coele-Syria and Palestine. The opportunity for cooperation arose for the Antigonid and Seleucid dynasties. The first four Ptolemaic rulers were always trying to prevent such cooperation, but now the worst-case scenario for them had come about. It is possible that the significance of this cooperation between Philip and Antiochus was exaggerated by historians, but it is certain that it involved at least a mutual non-intervention pact.

Antiochus III was finally able to occupy Coele-Syria and Palestine in 199. The Seleucid forces did not meet any serious resistance until they reached Gaza. They did claim the city by autumn but had to defend it against Ptolemaic counterattacks. By 199, Coele-Syria and Palestine were no longer under Ptolemaic rule. A Seleucid administration took over these lands almost immediately. It is not known how this change in regime affected the citizens of Syria, but there are documents confirming some prominent families who had served Ptolemy IV changed sides and received military commands under the new Seleucid administration.

While Antiochus III enjoyed his reign over Coele-Syria and Palestine, Philip V managed to provoke both the government of Rhodes and Attalus I (the king of Pergamon), who joined forces in a coalition. Philip didn't pay much attention to Rome at the time, even though Rome just signed a treaty in Africa signifying the end of their war with Hannibal and Carthage. While Philip was occupied in Caria (a region of western Anatolia), Attalus and Rhodes asked Rome for help to persuade Philip to quit his plans of asserting dominion in the Aegean. Rome sent an envoy whose task was to demand Philip immediately cease his attacks on the Greek cities and compensate

Attalus for the damage they endured. They even threatened with Roman intervention if Philip did not comply.

Philip was unimpressed by the Roman ultimatum, and he ordered an attack on Attica. He himself went toward the Dardanelles, taking over all the Ptolemaic towns and forts on the way. In Rome, a motion for war against Macedonia passed in the Senate. Publius Sulpicius Galba Maximus, an experienced consul, received the command, and by summer of 200, he had crossed the Adriatic Sea with a large fleet and army containing two full legions. This marked the beginning of the Second Macedonian War. The Roman army decided to build its base in Illyria, but part of the fleet went on and raided Philip's fortress of Chalcis. The Romans also raided some of the territories of Upper Macedonia. The Roman threat was serious, and their goal was to dismantle the dominance Macedonia had over southern Greece. It is clear that Rome wanted to dismantle the political structure of Macedonia as it represented a serious threat to them, and the Macedonian alliance fell apart under the pressure of the Roman threat.

The Romans promised a protectorate to the Greeks, thus selling them the war against Philip. Titus Quinctius Flamininus, a new commander, extended this protectorate with the demand that Philip needed to evacuate the whole of Greece. The Roman Senate declared all mainland and Ionian Greek cities free in 196, but it was clear that the stability of the Greek states wasn't immediate. In 194, Flamininus declared victory, and the Roman troops left the Greek states. The Greeks were now able to test the boundaries of their newly acquired freedom, and they could start a new political life. Rome was now considered to be a Hellenistic power, and the Greeks had to find a way to integrate that power into their own sociopolitical life.

In 200 and 199, Galba had devised a plan to attack Macedonia directly with the help of the Aetolian League, but the league showed little interest in joining the Romans. Galba failed to provoke Philip by attacking the territories of Upper Macedonia. However, Galba's successor, Flamininus, managed to secure an alliance with the Aetolians and with the Achaean League. Together, they struck hard against the Macedonian position in southern Greece and created a major breach.

Philip was now abandoned by his allies from the Achaean League, who favored Roman politics. Other allies soon followed, including Nabis, the ruler of Sparta. These new allies that Rome had suddenly gathered against Philip were demanding security for their own interests. At the gathering of the forces at Nikaia, in November 198, they all showed their own priorities. Flamininus revealed that Rome wanted certain Illyrian possessions that were under Philip. They also demanded that Ptolemy V retrieve all the territories that Philip took from him. Attalus demanded that Philip release the ships and crews he had captured in the Battle of Chios in 201. The Rhodians wanted Philip's current possessions in Asia Minor and on the Dardanelles. The Achaeans demanded Corinth and Argos, and the Aetolians wanted back all the territories they ever held. The demands were overwhelming.

Philip did not want to negotiate, however. He chose to fight a major battle that would decide his fate instead. He gathered an army with every man over sixteen and started to march toward Thessaly in 197. However, near Pherae, Philip's army was blocked by Flamininus and his allies. The battle took place at Cynoscephalae. Philip's army was practically annihilated, and it was only after this defeat that Philip agreed to negotiate.

The amount of power Rome now held over Greece became more visible, and as a result, peace was enforced. The final decision on how to proceed and which ally would get which of the retrieved territories laid completely in the hands of Rome. Rome did not want to dismantle and divide all the Macedonian territories between the Greeks. Instead, they argued that Macedonia had to continue functioning as a singular state in order to help defend against the northern non-Greek tribes. The Aetolians were not satisfied with this, and they demanded a reward because they played a major role in the battle against Philip.

The Roman Senate sent ten delegates to Greece to help Flamininus settle all of the questions. The decision of what to do with Philip and all the territories he once possessed was solely up to Rome, and so, Rome was about to redefine the Hellenistic state structure and status in Europe and in some parts of Asia. In Greece in the winter of 197, a *senatus consultum* (decree) took effect. Its purpose was to oversee the freedom of all the territories in Greece. However, the Aetolian League was still not satisfied. They were angry for not getting all the lands they were promised, and they started proclaiming that they had overthrown Philip just to be dominated by Rome now and that "Greek freedom" was nothing more than a farce.

In 196, Antiochus III crossed the Dardanelles and took over the city of Lysimachia, a city that had been recently evacuated by Philip. He also took Abydos, where Philip had a garrison. Rome didn't like this, as they considered it their duty to liberate any city where Philip had a military base. Flamininus took the opportunity during the international games in the summer of 196 to proclaim Rome's political statement. All lands south of Macedonia were to be without Roman garrisons and without taxes, and they had the freedom of enjoying their own laws and ways of life. Further, Rome demanded that Antiochus abandon all lands that used to be Ptolemaic or Antigonid. He was also prohibited from entering Europe with an army (which he already did) or attacking any of the Greek cities. Antiochus replied to these demands saying that Rome had no right to meddle in Asia, just as he would never meddle in the politics of Italy. As for the Ptolemaic lands, he answered that he was going to marry his own daughter to Ptolemy V, so that agenda was becoming a family matter and Rome cannot interfere. Antiochus never got an answer from Rome concerning these issues, and he did not have any contact with Rome for the next two years.

The Aetolian League was given some of the lands they asked for but not all. They were not satisfied, but they complained only verbally, taking no actions. They wanted the Thessalian cities most of all, but those were reorganized into a new league of their own, which was called the Thessalian League.

Rome's army was idle in the Greek states, so Flamininus decided it was time to return the troops to Rome. The Greek states showed their thanks to Rome, and 114 Greek communities presented their gifts to Flamininus and the Roman administration. These presents included tons of gold and silver, artworks of all kind, and freed Italian slaves who had been serving in the Greek cities since Hannibal had imprisoned them. Flamininus himself was celebrated in some Greek cities, and statues of him were erected. These thanksgiving celebrations were very popular for the next two centuries. Instating these thanksgiving celebrations, the Macedonian rulers showed their ability to adjust and accommodate to a new superpower, namely Rome.

Chapter 15 – Antiochus III and Rome

Timeline:

> 1. 192: Achaean League and Sparta at war; Nabis was betrayed and assassinated by the Aetolian League
> 2. 190: Battle of Myonnesus; Rome defeats Antiochus III

In 193, Antiochus III married his daughter, Cleopatra I, to Ptolemy V, thus settling the dispute over the Ptolemaic possessions in Syria. Antiochus saw himself as the only remaining major Macedonian power in the east. Because of this, he considered himself a Roman friend and equal. He sought to make an official alliance with Rome which would confirm and recognize his status.

Antiochus sent two representatives to Rome whose task was to persuade the Senate to abandon all interests they might have in Asia Minor and to seek friendship. They were unsatisfied as Flamininus declared that Antiochus needed to stay out of Europe if he wanted Rome to keep out of Asia Minor. Three Roman senators were sent to negotiate this personally with Antiochus.

While all of this happened in Rome, back home, Antiochus III was making large changes in his own kingdom. His eldest son, also named Antiochus, was given recognition as the heir apparent and was given the responsibility of the Upper Satrapies. He also started a cult dedicated to his wife, who was also his sister, Laodice IV. The true intention behind this was to force the elite citizens of the empire into loyalty through religious activities. Only the Macedonian aristocratic ladies of high status were chosen as priestesses for the newly founded cult, and Laodice actually became the high priestess of her own cult.

By the time the Roman senators reached Antiochus, his son and heir died. As he was in deep mourning, he couldn't receive Rome's representatives himself, so instead, he appointed a trusted courtier named Minnion to represent him. Minnion was sure that if the war between Rome and Antiochus was to happen, his king would be victorious. This gave him an aggressive stance in negotiations, and no compromise on the diplomatic issue was achieved.

At the same time, the unsatisfied Aetolians started sending messengers to Nabis of Sparta, to Philip V, and to Antiochus III with anti-Roman propaganda. A new war started in late 192 when Nabis, encouraged by the Aetolians, tried to retake Gythium, the main Spartan port which Flamininus gave to the Achaeans to supervise. Flamininus called for a truce, which Nabis accepted in order to gain time and ask the Aetolians for help. However, they were disappointed in Nabis' ineffectiveness and decided to assassinate him and take Sparta for themselves. The Spartans put up a strong resistance and nearly killed off all the Aetolian troops. The battle resulted in the Spartans choosing an Achaean-friendly government followed by them joining the league.

The situation in northern and central Greece, where the Aetolians were, was becoming much more serious for Rome. The Aetolian *strategos* Thoas gave Rome the idea that Antiochus' intention was to come to Greece to support the Aetolians. At the same time, he messaged Antiochus saying that the Balkan Greeks were waiting for him to come and free them from Rome. At that time, Rome had no troops in the Balkans, and Antiochus felt safe with his 10,000 men, which included 500 cavalry units and six war elephants. However, the Greeks didn't want to replace Rome with Antiochus, and the diplomacy that took place between them was hard on both sides. Chalcis refused to be liberated by Antiochus, so he decided to liberate it by force. He did this with many cities in the area, and these actions didn't paint a good image of Antiochus. Some places were more enthusiastic about him, and they accepted Seleucid garrisons without resistance. The Achaean League and Flamininus refused to recognize Antiochus' liberation actions, and they declared war.

Antiochus settled in Chalcis over winter, where he enjoyed his new marriage to a daughter of a local citizen. During spring, the Roman consul's army crossed the Adriatic under the command of Manius Acilius Glabrio. On their march toward Thessaly, this army accepted the surrender from all the cities Antiochus previously liberated. Antiochus was surprised by Rome's initiative and decided to take a stand and defend himself at the pass of Thermopylae, the same pass that the Spartan king Leonidas chose as a defense point against the Persian Empire. The Aetolians were also surprised by this turn of events and sent 4,000 men to help Antiochus, but half of these men set off to defend Heraclea instead, another Aetolian city. Antiochus was greatly outnumbered and stood no chance. Marcus Porcius Cato marched his troops and attacked Antiochus from the rear, thus crushing his resistance. Antiochus retreated to Ephesus.

Philip V offered the Romans help in logistics and as a reward recovered his son, who had been held as a hostage for five years, Demetrius. Rome demanded the Aetolians to surrender unconditionally, but they resisted. In 189, after three years of constant fighting, the Aetolians lost Ambracia. This event crushed their spirit, and they finally accepted Roman terms. The Aetolians had to pay restitution of 500 talents, and they were banned from expanding their league at the cost of Roman territories or territories belonging to Rome's friends. They were also banned from having an independent foreign policy, and they had to agree to have the same allies and enemies as Rome. This agreement was ratified by the Senate in 188, and the Aetolian League stopped being considered a major power in the Hellenistic world after this.

In addition, Rome restructured the state system of Asia Minor by bringing disaster on the Seleucid dynasty. Antiochus III didn't just help the Aetolians in their dissatisfaction with Rome; he also gave asylum to Hannibal, and this proved to be the main catalyst for prolonging the war. Rome now decided to put a stop on such ideas that anyone could be equal in power to them. Rome now had an interest in Asia Minor, and they had received support in this matter from Attalus I and later from his successor, Eumenes II of Pergamon, as well as Rhodes and all the cities which had appealed to Rome back in 197.

Finally, in 190, Lucius Cornelius Scipio and his more famous brother, Publius Cornelius Scipio Africanus (the man who defeated Hannibal in Africa), led the army into the territories of Asia Minor. The Roman fleet defeated Antiochus' fleet at Myonnesus near Samos and cut off Antiochus' troops who had stayed in Lysimachia. Antiochus tried to arrange negotiations with Rome, but they demanded him to evacuate Asia Minor north and west of the Taurus Mountains. They also demanded payment for all Roman war expenses. Seleucid pride made Antiochus refuse Rome's demands and instead engage in battle. At this point, even a defeat would bring him more prestige than just simply accepting Rome's terms. Antiochus gathered an army of between 50,000 to 70,000 men from every corner of his empire. He decided that the command of such an army should belong to himself and his son, Seleucus IV, who was his new heir. Rome sent four legions against him. Together with some allied forces, they had between 30,000 and 50,000 men. However, when it finally came to battle, Rome devastated Antiochus' army. The battle was fought near Magnesia by Sipylos in December 190. The Seleucid forces had around 50,000 dead and captured, according to the historians of the time (around 10,000 according to modern historians), which demonstrates the magnitude of Rome's victory. Antiochus, like Philip before him, had no other choice but to accept Rome's terms. The peace talks took place in Apamea in Phrygia, where it was decided that after ninety years of rule in the area, the Seleucids were to evacuate the rich territories north and west of the Taurus Mountains and give them to Rome's allies, Pergamon and Rhodes. About three years after the battle, Antiochus III died, leaving the Seleucid kingdom to his son, Seleucus IV.

In 179, Philip V also died. He was a witness to Macedonia being reduced to the status of a regional authority within the Hellenistic world. Philip underestimated the power of Rome, and he was the first to taste Rome's hostility. Although he respected the postwar treaty of friendship with Rome, Macedonia never enjoyed Rome's trust. In fact, Rome made sure that Macedonia wouldn't have any influence outside its own borders again.

Philip appointed his son Perseus as his successor, who had been trained in Macedonian politics. However, Rome favored his younger son, Demetrius, who had been kept as a hostage and had made contacts with Roman officials and learned how to navigate their political world. Perseus became king after his father passed, but he never really stood a chance. In 171, Rome attacked Macedonia, which started the Third (and final) Macedonian War. While Perseus requested negotiations, all of his efforts were ignored by Rome.

The real reason why Rome abolished the Macedonian monarchy in 168 is still unknown, but it is certain that making Macedonia a Roman province was the ultimate goal of the war. The Third Macedonian War lasted until 168 when the decisive Battle of Pydna was fought in Lower Macedonia. Afterward, the Macedonian kingdom was split into four republics.

Chapter 16 – Rome and Hellenistic Europe

Timeline:

1. 151: War between Sparta and the Achaean League
2. 146: Athens becomes tax-free city
3. 88: Mithridates VI attacks Roman province of Asia

The next quarter-century was about testing how much Rome was committed to the Greek world. By the mid-160s, Rome was recognized everywhere as a dominant power of the Hellenistic era.

The effects of Macedonia's fall were felt in Europe first. Aside from abolishing the Macedonian monarchy, the territory was split into four geographic units, known only by numbers instead of names. They were governed by a representative council, and they had no economic, social, or military collaborations between themselves. Due to the rise of violence and the rise of a certain Andriscus, who claimed to be the son of Perseus, Rome instituted a strict supervision system on all four Macedonian geographical units. This is how Macedonia came to be directly ruled as a provincial territory of Rome in 148, when the Roman praetor, Quintus Caecilius Metellus, defeated Andriscus, ending the Fourth Macedonian War. Macedonia finally ceased to be a Hellenistic state.

Among the allied Greek states, Rome made a difference between those that were dedicated to them and those that were unreliable. They asked for each state to make a list of unreliable men who could not be trusted, and they were taken to Rome as hostages. The Achaeans alone sent around 1,000 men. This was to ensure a pro-Roman political attitude to reduce any possible tensions. But since there was no permanent Roman presence in the area of the Greek free city-states, its leaders, though pro-Rome oriented, often ignored the Senate's decisions and resorted to violence to settle local disputes.

One such local dispute concerned Achaea and culminated into open warfare. The Spartans didn't want to be in the Achaean League, and in the year 151, Sparta challenged the Achaean League's jurisdiction in local city affairs. Achaean officials responded to the challenge with military preparations. Rome sent envoys to investigate the matter, but it took them eighteen months to arrive. In that time, the war was already raging. Roman senators failed to solve the problem in Sparta, resulting in Achaea's military attack.

The Achaean War in 146 left European Greece in ruins, and it ended independent political activity in the Greek states. The Achaean League was reduced to a small state, but Sparta and Messene were finally free, as long as their behavior satisfied Rome. Rome at this time didn't think it was necessary to make a province out of the southern Greek states, but it did ensure they pay taxes, and the proconsul of provincial Macedonia had to supervise the administration.

Athens was the only European state who had profited from the Third Macedonian War. They were considered militarily and politically too weak, but after the war, Rome gifted them a group of islands, including the sacred island of Delos. In 146, Athens instituted their own administration on this island, and it flourished because Rome allowed it to have a tax-free status. Because of Roman support, Athens once again became successful. This symbiosis of the Greek state and Roman power resulted in the flourishing of culture.

However, it only lasted until Athens chose to abandon Roman generosity and give open support to the Pontic king, Mithridates VI, when he attacked a Roman province of Asia in 88. Athenian citizens on Delos remained loyal to Rome, as they were aware of who they owed their prosperity to. Because of this loyalty, the island was devastated by Mithridates' general, Archelaus. However, Athens itself now became the main objective for the Roman legions, under the command of Lucius Cornelius Sulla. The siege of Athens ended in a bloodbath when the Roman troops penetrated the city on March 1, 86. Athens did not try to be independent ever again, as they were not able to recover from the war. Delos, on the other hand, just started to prosper again when it was ransacked by pirates in 69. After the raid, Delos stopped being the commercial heart of Roman Greece.

Chapter 17 – Rome in Egypt and Asia

Timeline:

1. 196: Crowning of Ptolemy V in Memphis
2. 194: Ptolemy V marries Cleopatra I
3. 180: Death of Ptolemy V
4. 176: Death of Cleopatra I
5. 175: Antiochus IV becomes the ruler of the Seleucid Empire
6. 169: War starts between the Seleucid and Ptolemaic Empires
7. 168: Battle of Pydna
8. 164: Death of Antiochus IV
9. 160: Death of Judas Maccabaeus
10. 141: Independence of Judaea

The early years of the second century brought stability in Ptolemaic Egypt without any influence from Rome. This improvement of stability is associated with Polycrates of Argos, a senior officer who managed to put an end to the rebellions occurring in Egypt. The child king Ptolemy V was crowned in November of 196, in Memphis when he was only fourteen. It took another decade before the rebellion in Upper Egypt could be stopped. The first problem to be dealt with after regaining these areas was normalizing the operation of agriculture, which was the backbone of the Egyptian economy.

In 194, Cleopatra I, daughter of Antiochus III, married Ptolemy V, and this event is considered to be pivotal for the future of Egypt. Antiochus gave his daughter in the hopes of keeping Coele-Syria under Seleucid control, but later, Ptolemaic revanchists claimed it was part of Cleopatra's dowry. As long as Ptolemy and Cleopatra lived, Coele-Syria remained under Seleucid control, and these two dynasties lived in peace. Ptolemy V died of poisoning in 180, leaving two sons and a daughter who were all too young to take the throne. Cleopatra I was a rather effective regent for her son, Ptolemy VI, until her death in 176. Afterward, Egypt was left to survive on the ability of regents Eulaeus and Lenaeus, who failed to fulfill their purpose. Egypt's regents wanted to retrieve Coele-Syria but failed, threatening the independence of all of Egypt. Roman intervention was needed in order to save Egypt.

Ptolemy VI Philometor, the elder son of Ptolemy V, married his sister, Cleopatra II, in 173 in efforts to stop sibling rivalry. Then Egypt tried to invade Syria, but Antiochus IV, the current ruler of the Seleucid Empire, marched into Egypt and defeated the Egyptian army near the town of Pelusium. Negotiations started, and an agreement was reached that Antiochus IV be proclaimed as the protector of Ptolemy VI, as Antiochus was his uncle. However, the Alexandrian court refused to accept this agreement and proclaimed the younger brother, Ptolemy VIII, to be the ruler. Antiochus started the siege of Alexandria in 169, and even though the government appealed to Rome, they had to wait for a response until the spring of 168.

Ptolemy agreed to unite with his siblings in efforts against Antiochus. By the spring of 168, Antiochus controlled large parts of Lower Egypt, but Rome finally sent word. A group of *legati* (ambassadors) led by Gaius Popillius Laenas was sent to intervene in Egypt, and they brought Rome's ultimatum to Antiochus: He was to leave Egypt immediately. Popillius did not offer enough time for Antiochus to think about the situation. Instead, he drew his men into a circle around the king and told him that he would not be able to leave until he made a decision. By July 30, 168, Antiochus' troops left Egypt. These events mark Ptolemaic recognition of Rome's ever-growing power.

After Antiochus IV withdrew from Egypt, Coele-Syria remained in his hands. But soon after, Jewish territories, under the leadership of Judas Maccabaeus of the Hasmonean family, started resisting Seleucid rule. Their ultimate goal was to create an independent Jewish state in Palestine. The financial interests of Antiochus IV were the cause of the first conflict he had with Jewish establishments. He needed money to pay Rome, and Jewish settlements were a good resource as they paid no taxes to the Seleucid rulers due to an agreement with Antiochus III in 200 when he took over Coele-Syria. On his way back from Egypt, Antiochus IV entered Jerusalem with his army and took funds from Jewish temple treasures. This plundering of sacred temples ignited their resistance to the Seleucid royal authority.

In order to stop Jewish uprisings, Antiochus prohibited the practice of their faith and attempted to force the Jewish people to make sacrifices to Zeus. Those who disobeyed and continued practicing Judaism were persecuted. In autumn of 164, Antiochus suffered an accident and died, leaving behind a nine-year-old son, Antiochus V, as his successor. Syrian Chancellor Lysias controlled the new boy king, and the first thing he set out to do was restore order in Jerusalem by returning the Jewish way of life to the city. But it was too late. The Maccabaean resistance did not want peace, as it would only mean returning under Seleucid rule. Their aim was to create an independent state of Judaea. In 161, before his death, Judas Maccabaeus managed to convince Rome to recognize the separate political entity of the Jewish population, even though they were still officially part of the Seleucid monarchy.

Seleucus IV's son Demetrius I Soter had been held as a hostage in Rome since 175, but he freed himself and escaped Italy in 162. He then assassinated Antiochus V and his advisor Lysias and took the throne. Demetrius I continued to pursue the renegade Jewish leaders, and in 160, he managed to kill Judas. Afterward, a peace followed, which the Jewish used to reorganize their forces.

Demetrius was killed in 150 by Alexander Balas, who claimed to be the son of Antiochus IV and enjoyed the support of Rome. Balas claimed the throne and married Ptolemy VI's daughter, Cleopatra Thea. Ptolemy managed to recover Coele-Syria from the Seleucids but provoked Alexander Balas, who tried to assassinate him. As a result, Ptolemy took back his daughter and offered her and his support to Demetrius II, son of Demetrius I. Ptolemy may have died while confronting Balas, but Balas was assassinated shortly after, thus leaving the Seleucid possessions in the hands of the young and inexperienced Demetrius II. The Jewish leader, Jonathan Apphus (Judas' brother), exploited Demetrius' inexperience and convinced him to confirm Jewish privileges, even managing to extend those privileges.

A new Jewish leader, Simon Thassi, another one of Judas' brothers, succeeded in expelling the Seleucid garrison from Jerusalem, and in the year 141, he proclaimed the independence of the Hasmonean state of Judaea. Demetrius' younger brother, Antiochus VII, came to power in 138 and married Cleopatra Thea to gain the prestige of her dynasty. He is the one who managed to return Jerusalem under Seleucid rule in 131, but shortly after, he died in the decisive Battle of Ecbatana in 129 BCE when the Parthians conquered Iran once and for all from the Seleucids. His brother Demetrius II returned to power after being released from imprisonment.

With the death of Antiochus VII, the Seleucid monarchy stopped being an important power in the Hellenistic world. Reduced only to Syria, and without Judaea, the Seleucid kingdom was so weak that even Rome considered it unworthy of intervention. Cleopatra Thea had her own ambitions of becoming a sole ruler, however. She assassinated her eldest son who had tried to claim the throne. Her second son, Antiochus VIII Grypus, managed to claim the crown, and soon after, he poisoned Cleopatra, claiming she tried to assassinate him just as she did his brother. Grypus was defeated by his half-brother known as Antiochus IX, but by this point, all respect the Seleucids once enjoyed had been lost. Rome now decided Syria was too valuable to be left in the hands of incompetent rulers of Macedonian kingdoms, so they established direct Roman rule. Soon after, in 63 BCE, Syria finally became a Roman province under Gnaeus Pompeius Magnus, better known as Pompey, who defeated Mithridates VI. However, the city of Antioch enjoyed the status of a self-governing city and didn't have to pay taxes to Rome.

This is how the second Macedonian dynasty came to an end, leaving only the Ptolemaic dynasty left. Since the death of Antiochus IV, the Seleucids played dynastic power games, losing more and more territories of their kingdom and reducing it to a small, insignificant state without any influence in the Hellenistic world. What happened next in Syria was left to Rome to decide.

Chapter 18 – Hellenistic Anatolia Defeated

Timeline:

1. 120: Mithridates VI begins rule over Pontus
2. 95: Mithridates VI attacks Cappadocia
3. 85: Treaty of Dardanus
4. 83/82: Second Mithridatic War begins
5. 63: Third Mithridatic War ends

When the power of the Seleucids and Ptolemies had diminished, their administrative, cultural, and political traditions did not cease to exist. The Romans developed the old territories of great Macedonian kingdoms into new monarchies. Similar developments happened in eastern and central Anatolia, where the collapse of the Seleucid dynasty allowed the growth of new regional powers. Of great interest in this area was the Kingdom of Cappadocia, through which all communications between Syria and the Aegean passed.

The Roman presence in Asia Minor became significant, and it did not please the rulers of Bithynia, Cappadocia, and Pontus. All three of these states suddenly became the neighbors of the new Roman province of Asia. The death of king Mithridates V in 120 was a critical point for Asia Minor. He left two sons, Mithridates VI and Mithridates Chrestus, as joint rulers, with their mother, Laodice VI, acting as regent. Soon after, Mithridates VI threw his mother and brother in prison, where they would eventually die of natural causes, and began his sole rule. He was especially suspicious of Roman interests in Asia Minor, and he detested their presence in neighboring lands.

Mithridates VI was an aggressive ruler, and he was quick to attack Cappadocia and Paphlagonia. He managed to destabilize these states through a series of violent attacks as well as through diplomatic interventions. Cappadocia was friendly toward Rome, and their ruler, Ariarathes VII, led a traditional policy of being Roman allies. When Mithridates killed Ariarathes and continued his quarrel with Nicomedes III of Bithynia, his main rival, Rome felt obligated to intervene; after all, it was their neighboring states that were fighting, and it was only a matter of time before they would extend their conquest toward the Roman province. They called both kings to cease the attacks, and they declared Cappadocia to be a free state. However, Cappadocia wanted a king and voted for Ariobarzanes I, a Cappadocian noble, as their new king in 95. The Roman Senate supported this decision.

But Mithridates VI himself never abandoned the idea of conquering Bithynia. Nicomedes IV, the new king of Bithynia, supported by Rome, started attacking his territories. In 89, Mithridates won a decisive battle against the Roman and Bithynian forces in Pontus. Afterward, he started preparing for an aggressive war. In 88, he attacked Cappadocia and Bithynia, thus meddling in Roman interests in Asia. However, Rome was still strong, and by the end of this war, they confirmed their hold on the provinces of Asia and the Balkans, where Mithridates sent his general Archelaus to fight.

Lucius Cornelius Sulla brought peace through negotiations in 85 at Dardanus. Mithridates had to withdraw from the Greek mainland, Aegean islands, Bithynia, Paphlagonia, Phrygia, and Cappadocia, but he was allowed to continue ruling Pontus. Nicomedes and Ariobarzanes were reinstated as kings of their lands, and Mithridates was given a chance to fight another day. Sulla needed peace at that time because a civil war in Italy was about to start, and he had to concentrate all his efforts back home.

In 83 or 82, the Second Mithridatic War began when Lucius Licinius Murena, Sulla's lieutenant, attacked Mithridates. Less than ten years later, Nicomedes IV, who had succeeded his father, Nicomedes III, on the throne of Bithynia in 94, died and left his kingdom to the people of Rome in his will. Rome didn't waste time and immediately organized this new territory as a province. Mithridates couldn't bear the thought of having the Roman province of Bithynia as a neighbor, so he decided to attack it by land and sea. The Roman authorities were surprised by this attack but managed to regain full control and prove to Mithridates that his decision was a disastrous one.

Rome decided that Mithridates had to be eliminated and stopped responding to negotiation attempts. Pontus occupied a large mountainous area in eastern Anatolia, which slowed the progress of the Roman legions, thus prolonging the war. The Roman forces were led by Lucullus, Sulla's lieutenant who showed great effectiveness in the first war against Mithridates. In 73, Mithridates was cast out of Bithynia, and his fleet was destroyed at Lemnos. Lucullus and Mithridates confronted each other in the Battle of Cabira in 71 in central Pontus. Mithridates decided to retreat and escape to the Kingdom of Armenia, which was ruled by his son-in-law Tigranes II the Great. During the same year, Lucullus informed the Senate of his success in taking the royal residences Sinope and Amasya, and soon, the *legati* were sent to organize the new province. However, Mithridates was still on the loose, and in 67, he managed to raise a new army in Pontus and defeat the Roman army under Gaius Valerius Triarius at Zela. Once more, Mithridates proved he was a powerful man.

In 66, Pompey was appointed to deal with Mithridates once and for all. Lucullus was recalled, so Pompey took the rewards for all the achievements in Pontus. Mithridates was forced out of Pontus, and in his retreat, he arrived at the Cimmerian Bosporus where his son, Machares, ruled. His son was a friend of Rome but did not want to betray his own father, so he decided to commit suicide to escape the uncomfortable situation. Mithridates tried to gain control over his son's lands but was so brutal in his attempts that his son, Pharnaces II, led a rebellion against him. With nowhere else to turn, Mithridates committed suicide via his bodyguard striking him down.

Mithridates' son-in-law, Tigranes, in eastern Anatolia, decided to surrender to Pompey when he saw the display of the might and power of Rome. This moment placed all of Anatolia and Syria into Roman hands. Three territories, Armenia, Cappadocia, and the Bosporan Kingdom, had their own rulers recognized by Rome but were powerless and became satellite states of Rome. They stopped being Hellenistic states in all aspects at this point.

Chapter 19 – Rome in Egypt

Timeline:

1. 161: Ptolemy VIII attacks Cyprus
2. 145: Death of Ptolemy VI Philometor; Ptolemy VIII crowned as ruler and married to Cleopatra II
3. 132: Civil war in Egypt
4. 116: Death of Ptolemy VIII; crowning of Ptolemy IX; death of Cleopatra II
5. 107: Ptolemy X becomes king in Alexandria
6. 101: Death of Cleopatra III
7. 96: Death of Ptolemy Apion
8. 88: Ptolemy IX is restored as king of Egypt
9. 80: Death of Ptolemy IX; Ptolemy XI rules briefly before assassination; Ptolemy XII crowned
10. 58: Ptolemy XII deposed and flees to Rome
11. 55: Ptolemy XII restored as king of Egypt
12. 51: Death of Ptolemy XII; ascension of Cleopatra VII and Ptolemy XIII
13. 49-47: Civil war in Egypt
14. 48: Caesar comes to Alexandria
15. 44: Murder of Caesar; Cleopatra goes to Rome
16. 31: Battle of Actium
17. 30: Death of Cleopatra; end of Ptolemaic rule in Egypt

Ptolemaic Egypt was the longest surviving monarchy of the three Macedonian kingdoms of the post-Alexandrian age. Egypt was always a special case due to its physical distance from the center of Mediterranean affairs and because of its unique cultural identity. It never presented a threat to Roman interests until Cleopatra VII in 31 BCE.

The joint rule of Ptolemaic brothers and their sister Cleopatra II fell apart briefly in 164. Ptolemy VI and Cleopatra II were driven out of Egypt by their younger brother, Ptolemy VIII, and they sought refuge in Rome. Ptolemy VI managed to gain the support of some of the senators and was escorted back to Alexandria with Roman *legati* in 163. In one year of ruling on his own, the younger brother had become so unpopular that he gladly accepted the proposition of the Romans to give him rule over Cyrenaica.

Ptolemy VIII later launched two failed expeditions to conquer Cyprus from his siblings, and Ptolemy VIII asked Rome for help. It was granted but under the condition that there would be no war between them. Ptolemy VI refused to surrender Cyprus to his brother without a fight, and Rome retreated from these Egyptian efforts. In the end, Ptolemy VI agreed to give Ptolemy VIII control over Cyrenaica, thus showing goodwill and dispersing the rumors that he wanted to assassinate the younger Ptolemy. Ptolemy VI's biggest success was recovering Coele-Syria and returning it to Ptolemaic rule. But this success was interrupted by his death after a battle near Antioch in 145.

Ptolemy VI's death marks the start of the decline of Ptolemaic Egypt, which was eventually taken over by Rome. The inner dynastic struggles accompanied by civil wars became a dominant trait of Egyptian history. Cleopatra II wanted to rule by herself after her brother-husband's death (some believe he was murdered at Ptolemy VIII's command), but their younger brother saw an opportunity and came to Alexandria to establish himself as the king. The position of Cleopatra II became hopeless as she had no support left; she had to compromise and accept her younger brother in

101

marriage. Later, Ptolemy VIII decided to marry her teenage daughter from her previous marriage with their older brother and instituted her as a joint queen next to Cleopatra II. This second wife became known as Cleopatra III, and he married her in 139, without divorcing his first wife. The tension between the three rulers was so great that in 132 a civil war erupted between Cleopatra II and Ptolemy VIII with Cleopatra III as his supporter. Cleopatra II managed to raise so much support that her opponents had to flee Egypt.

Cleopatra II claimed to continue Ptolemy VI's traditional rule. She even took his old title (Philometor), and in addition, she used the cult title "Soteira" and tried to start a new dynasty. Ptolemy VIII murdered his own son, Ptolemy Memphites, whom he had with Cleopatra II, and sent his remains in a box to the queen on her birthday. This act made him extremely unpopular in Alexandria, but he still had supporters in the Egyptian countryside. The whole land was politically divided with Upper Egypt and Cyrenaica remaining loyal to Ptolemy VIII.

The dynastic turmoil continued after Ptolemy VIII's death in 116. He left two wills, the first stating that he was leaving Cyrenaica to Rome if he remained childless, which he did not. However, the second stated that he was leaving it to his illegitimate son, Ptolemy Apion. The second will proved to be ineffective. Ptolemy VIII treated the territories of Egypt as his own personal property, and he assumed he could decide who would inherit them. However, reality proved to be different. Cleopatra III favored her younger son as a successor of Ptolemy, but Cleopatra II was still alive, and she supported the tradition of the firstborn son being the official heir. At first, Cleopatra II was successful in her intention to put the elder son of Ptolemy VIII, on the throne as she had gained the support of Alexandria and its garrison troops.

The elder son, named Ptolemy IX, was crowned in Egypt, and Cleopatra II died later that year. The king's mother, Cleopatra III, insisted that he divorce his sister-wife, Cleopatra IV, in order to marry his younger sister, Cleopatra Selene I, which he did, but the date remains unknown.

Cleopatra III never abandoned her intention of proclaiming her younger son, Ptolemy X, to be king in Alexandria, and in 107, she finally succeeded. Ptolemy IX sought refuge in Cyprus. It is unclear how this change of rulers happened, but since Cleopatra III stayed a dominant figure in the Alexandrian court, it is likely that she was the one pushing for the change. Ptolemy Apion, Ptolemy VIII's illegitimate son, had been ruling Cyrenaica since 116 BCE. Ptolemy IX ruled Cyprus as a governor. From a certain perspective, the Ptolemaic Kingdom was now split in three parts, with Ptolemy IX ruling in Cyprus, Ptolemy Apion in Cyrene, and Ptolemy X in Alexandria.

What the Roman intentions were regarding Egypt during this period of the three kingdoms is uncertain. However, Rome recognized all three kings as legitimate and did not protest this split of Egypt. In 96, Ptolemy Apion died and chose to leave Cyrenaica to the Roman Republic as he had no heirs. Rome exploited the royal estates there, but the lands were not strategically important to them.

Not much is known of Ptolemy X's rule. He was unpopular with the people and melted the sarcophagus of Alexander the Great in order to repay the mercenaries he hired. He was expelled from Alexandria by the people, and his reign ended in 88. The next prominent figure from the dynasty was Cleopatra Berenice, also known as Berenice III, the wife of Ptolemy X and the daughter of his brother Ptolemy IX. Ptolemy IX came back to Alexandria to rule, and she became his queen.

The events that were to end the dynastic rule of Egypt were starting to culminate in Asia Minor. In 80, Ptolemy IX died, leaving the throne to Cleopatra Berenice. However, Rome had different intentions. Lucius Cornelius Sulla wanted a pro-Roman ruler on the throne and sent Ptolemy XI, who had been given to Rome during the peace negotiations between Mithridates VI and Rome in 85.

Mithridates had captured Ptolemy XI in 88, making him a perfect bargaining chip to use in the negotiations. In Rome's decision to make Ptolemy XI the new king of Egypt, he had to sign a will that stated that after his death his lands would belong to Rome. He also had to marry Cleopatra Berenice, who he killed after less than three weeks of marriage. But Cleopatra had been so popular amongst the people of Alexandria that the mob lynched their new king in revenge. Ptolemy XI was the last legitimate male ruler of the Ptolemy dynasty.

However, the Ptolemy dynasty didn't end. Soon after, two illegitimate sons of Ptolemy IX presented themselves and were placed to rule over Alexandria and Cyprus. Rome never recognized them officially as kings, but they also didn't oppose them. The king in Alexandria, known as Ptolemy XII, married his sister or possibly his cousin Cleopatra V Tryphaena, and together, they ruled for the next ten years. In 69, Cleopatra disappears from the royal records, but she wasn't dead.[2] In Rome, young Gaius Julius Caesar and Marcus Crassus were already plotting on how to take over Egypt. By the year 58, Cyprus was annexed as a Roman province.

In Alexandria, Ptolemy XII was not wanted as a ruler, and he begged Rome for military help against the revolting people of his capital. However, Alexandrians supported his former wife, Cleopatra Tryphaena, who declared her own daughter as joint queen, known as Berenice IV, in 57 (some historians believe that Berenice killed her in order to take the throne). Berenice eliminated her husband, Seleucus VII, son of Cleopatra Selene, and married Archelaus I, a high priest of Cappadocia who claimed to be the son of Mithridates VI. This joint rule didn't last long as Ptolemy XII was restored by Rome in 55. Berenice and Archelaus were killed, and Rome now had

---

[2] Historians cannot agree on what happened because there are several theories that include mentions of more than one Cleopatra. It is, in fact, possible that Cleopatra V died in 69. But it is also possible that she is later mentioned in the records under a different Cleopatra Tryphaena, Cleopatra VI.

direct interest in Egypt and appointed their own statesmen in key positions within the Egyptian court. A Roman garrison also remained present in Egypt. Ptolemy XII remained king of Egypt as a puppet of Rome until 51 when he died.

By the time Caesar's civil war began in Rome in 49, Egypt was part of the Roman Republic, but it was not yet declared a province. Egypt was treated as a satellite state of Rome and was directly involved in the civil war. When Ptolemy XII died in 51, his daughter, Cleopatra VII, became the joint ruler of Egypt with her brother, Ptolemy XIII. She was appointed as joint ruler with her father earlier, but his will left her as the successor even though he had male heirs. The copy of this will was sent to Rome to nullify the previous agreement that said Rome would inherit his lands after his death.

Cleopatra VII had to marry her younger brother, who was only ten years old at the time. The tensions in court continued as always with different sides supporting either Cleopatra or her brother. Soon, she was exiled to Syria, and her brother, Ptolemy XIII, was formally recognized by Rome as the king in Alexandria.

In Rome, civil war raged between Gaius Julius Caesar and Pompey, and in August 48, Pompey, the general who conquered Mithridates VI, was defeated. He retreated to Egypt, where he was surprised to find Cleopatra facing Ptolemy XIII with an army. Egyptian court advisors realized they were supporting the losing side of the Roman civil war and plotted to murder Pompey. His head was presented to Caesar when he arrived in Alexandria; however, he was incredibly displeased by this action. Caesar was so angry at the men responsible that he sought to avenge Pompey's death. It is not known in the records what happened to all the men involved, but at least one managed to escape.

Ptolemy's and Cleopatra's armies never had the chance to clash. Caesar ordered them dissolved and invited both Egyptian rulers before him. Because Cleopatra had been exiled during the Roman civil war, Caesar was under the impression that she supported him instead of Pompey, and she did nothing to discourage this thought. It was her chance, and she recognized it. However, Alexandria supported Ptolemy XIII and acted hostile toward Cleopatra and Caesar. As a result, fighting started between the Roman garrisons stationed there, and Ptolemy's troops, which were never dissolved like Caesar had ordered, joined the fight against them with the help of the Alexandrian population.

In 47, supported with troops from Syria, Caesar was victorious in the Battle of the Nile. Ptolemy XIII supposedly drowned while trying to escape from the battlefield. Cleopatra married her younger brother, known as Ptolemy XIV, who was just twelve at the time. This was done so that the people of Alexandria could be appeased because they did not like the idea of being ruled by a sole female ruler. This civil war in Egypt is typically remembered as the fight in which the Library of Alexandria was destroyed by fire. However, the library is mentioned in sources until the middle of the third century CE; it is far more likely that the library faded in importance and fell into disrepair over time.

Roman dominance over Egypt was obvious even though Caesar avoided annexing it as a Roman province. Cleopatra gave birth to a child whom she named Ptolemy Caesar after his father. But he was always known as Caesarion (Little Caesar). Caesar gave Cyprus back to Cleopatra, but she had to give him all its incomes if he demanded it.

Caesar was murdered on March 15, 44. At that time, Cleopatra and her son were living in Rome but had to go back to Alexandria, where she assassinated her own brother and appointed her son as joint ruler.

In 42 BCE, following the Battle of Philippi, Marcus Antonius, more commonly known as Mark Antony, and Gaius Octavianus, better known as Octavian, and Lepidus divided the Roman Republic between themselves, with Antony becoming the new ruler in the Eastern Empire. Cleopatra knew she had to win him over, just like she had with Caesar. Egypt became a secure base for Antony, and

Cleopatra provided him with whatever he needed for his efforts in eastern Anatolia. With him, she had three children over the next years. Their love has been romanticized in culture, but in reality, she had no choice but to support the Roman side, as they had the power over her lands. In 31, Antony lost the civil war in a final battle against Octavian at Actium. The following year, Octavian came to Alexandria and officially ended the Ptolemaic dynasty's rule over Egypt. Cleopatra committed suicide, and Caesarion was murdered. Her other children were brought to Rome to be presented as Octavian's triumph over Egypt. The last great Macedonian monarchy had come to an end.

Chapter 20 – Rome's Path to Power

Timeline:

1. 264-241: First Punic War
2. 218-201: Second Punic War
3. 202: Battle of Zama
4. 149-146: Third Punic War
5. 135: First slave uprising
6. 85: Peace between Lucius Cornelius Sulla and Mithridates VI
7. 78: Death of Sulla
8. 73-71: Third slave uprising
9. 60-53: First Triumvirate
10. 49: Start of Caesar's civil war
11. 48: Death of Gnaeus Pompeius Magnus (Pompey the Great)
12. 45: End of Caesar's civil war
13. 44: Assassination of Caesar
14. 43-33: Second Triumvirate
15. 31: Battle of Actium
16. 30: Octavian in Egypt; end of Ptolemaic Egypt

To understand the influence and significance Rome had on the Hellenistic world and vice versa, a reflection must be made on Rome itself. After the death of Alexander the Great, Rome was nothing more than a formal capital of the Latin League. But its growth was quick. Influenced by Greeks, Latins, and Etruscans, Rome reorganized their religion and politics. It was ruled by oligarchs who monopolized every segment of the state, and at the top of the government, there were two consuls with extensive power in politics and religion; the consuls, unlike the oligarch, were elected every year. To rule their newly conquered provinces, the Romans had to organize promagistrates, proconsuls, and propraetors who became the governors of new territories during Roman expansion. During the early Hellenistic age, Rome was going through the period of constructing itself as a republic.

For the whole existence of the republic, Rome was in a constant state of war, showing its resilience and ability to quickly recover from any significant losses. In 387, the Gauls ransacked Rome, but the recovery was so quick that Rome managed to conquer the whole Italian peninsula and present itself as a new, formidable power in the Mediterranean. It all happened in a span of just one century, bringing great military recognition to Rome.

Wars of the Roman Republic

The greatest enemy of the Roman Republic was Carthage. While the Hellenistic states were being divided by Alexander's heirs, Rome was just entering the Punic Wars, the largest wars ever to be fought at that time.

The cause of the wars was Rome's tendency to expand on any of the territories of Carthage, mainly Sicily. It took three great wars for Rome to establish its dominance. At first, Carthage had the naval advantage over Rome, and they won the Battle of the Lipari Islands in 260. But once again, Rome showed its ability to overcome the situation. They expanded and rebuilt their navy, and in less than two months, they had over a hundred warships ready for battle. The First Punic War (264-241) ended with Rome winning a streak of battles and forcing Carthage to sign a peace treaty in which they had to pay a significant amount of money to Rome as war indemnity. This brought destabilization to Carthage, which eventually led to the Second Punic War.

The Second Punic War (218-201) was mostly remembered because of the famous Carthaginian general Hannibal Barca, who crossed the Alps and invaded Italy from the north. Hannibal is still considered one of the greatest military commanders throughout history. He won some of the major battles of this period, but he never managed to break the bond between Rome and its allies, which eventually led to his demise. At the same time as the Second Punic War, Rome was also at war with Philip V of Macedonia, who allied himself with Hannibal. Rome had no intention of expanding to Macedonia, but they had to keep Philip V occupied on one front while fighting Carthage on what they considered to be the main front. Rome could not risk Philip V sending reinforcements to Hannibal as that would enable him to conquer the city itself. Rome was under siege but endured, and even though Hannibal begged Carthage to send help, the army never arrived, and he had to rely on his political ability to separate Rome from its allies. But aside from some southern city-states, Rome's allies chose to fight alongside their partner, supplying the city with much-needed food, resources, and soldiers.

Hannibal sustained his forces in Italy for fifteen years, but he felt compelled to turn back and defend his territory in Africa when Rome attacked it. Hannibal suffered a major defeat at the Battle of Zama in 202, which marked the end of the Second Punic War. Hannibal was defeated by the Roman general Scipio Africanus, who is still considered to be one of the greatest Roman military commanders.

For over fifty years, there was peace between Rome and Carthage, but that doesn't mean war didn't happen on other fronts. When Philip V of Macedonia died, his heir, Perseus of Macedonia, tried to expand his international influence, and he was aggressive about it, moving against his own neighbors who were allies of Rome. Rome had to respond, and the Roman Senate officially declared war on

Macedonia. This was when Rome came to the conclusion that it needed a permanent base in the Greek world.

Hannibal continued to act in Carthage but this time as a politician. He reorganized the state's finances, paid war indemnity to Rome, and fought corruption amongst his fellow state officials. Rome saw his activities as a sign of collaboration with Antiochus III of the Seleucid Empire, who was, at the time, an enemy. Because of these accusations, Hannibal chose voluntary exile in 195 to avoid being handed over to the Romans. The exact age and cause of his death are unknown, but Hannibal never again returned to Carthage.

While Rome fought wars in Macedonia, Carthage had time to recover, and in the fifty years of peacetime, they had reorganized their navy and paid their war debt to Rome. However, Rome believed otherwise and made a set of demands Carthage could not possibly fulfill. One of the demands was to completely demolish the city and rebuild it deeper off the coast of Africa. When this demand was refused, Rome declared the Third Punic War against Carthage. The Roman commander Scipio Aemilianus besieged the city for three years. After finally breaching the walls, he ransacked the city and burned it completely in 146. The remaining citizens of Carthage were sold into slavery, and the remaining territories became known as the Roman province of Africa.

Civil Wars

The rapid expansion of Rome took a toll on its social organization. The very heart of the Roman Republic was pressured by political violence and slave uprisings. This period is known for some of the most famous men in history, such as Julius Caesar, Gaius Marius, and Lucius Cornelius Sulla, to name a few.

The first slave uprising took place in 135 and was led by Eunus and Cleon. It took three years for consul Publius Rupilius to successfully end this rebellion. This event led to various senators trying to change the very foundation of the Roman Republic and pass the laws that would limit individual wealth and owned territories. The end goal of these political moves was to weaken the Senate's power and introduce a more democratic approach to solving state problems. Over the span of a few decades, these reorganizations took place in the Roman Senate. Some were successful, some less so, but they contributed to the instability in the core of Roman society, dividing senators and consuls who had no choice but to gather around one prominent figure and act as his supporter.

Two significant social wars broke out between the supporters of Gaius Marius, a very distinctive military commander who became consul, and Lucius Cornelius Sulla. Sulla was a leader of a political faction of Rome known as the *Optimates*. Their agenda was to keep senatorial power intact and fight against social reforms proposed by the faction led by Gaius Marius, the *Populares*. Because of the dispute regarding who would take leadership in the war against Mithridates VI, Sulla decided to attack the army led by Gaius Marcius Censorinus. The battle took place in 88 at the very door of Rome; however, there wasn't much of a battle to speak of. Sulla was victorious, but his actions started the era of civil wars where Rome's armies fought against each other. These civil wars ultimately led to the end of the Roman Republic and the foundation of the Roman Empire.

After taking Rome, Sulla decided to go back to war with Mithridates VI. Gaius Marius took the opportunity of Sulla's absence and established himself in Rome once again. In 85, Sulla made peace with Mithridates and returned to Rome. He managed to overcome all resistance from the opposing party of Gaius Marius and retake the city with his army. He slaughtered most of Gaius' supporters and proclaimed himself dictator in order to strengthen the aristocracy and the Senate. He made a series of reforms, resigned the dictatorship, and became a consul one last time before his death in 78.

Another significant event that shook the very foundation of Rome was the third slave uprising, which lasted from 73 until 71. It was led by the famous Spartacus, and it involved about 120,000 escaped slaves and gladiators, including non-combatants. At the same time, a civil war in Hispania took place as well, and two prominent commanders of Sulla's party were sent to put them down. Gnaeus Pompeius Magnus (Pompey the Great) was sent to Hispania, and Marcus Licinius Crassus was appointed to deal with the uprising of Spartacus. Both generals were eventually successful. Upon their return to Rome, they joined forces and made a deal with the *Populares* party, which elected both generals as consuls. Now they had the power to dismantle Sulla's constitution.

Through a series of political events, mainly performed by Marcus Tullius Cicero, the famed statesman, philosopher, and consul, the political party *Populares* was dismantled, and Pompey was left without power in Rome. He was approached by Gaius Julius Caesar, who offered a private political agreement between the two of them and Marcus Licinius Crassus. This agreement is known as the First Triumvirate. The agreement stated that Pompey's efforts in Asia would be ratified by the Senate (something the Senate avoided doing), and in return, Caesar would be elected as consul in 59. Crassus, the third member of the Triumvirate, was promised a senatorial seat sometime in the future. Crassus was previously Caesar's patron in all but name. He financed his political campaigns and was his most obvious supporter. He was also known as the "richest man in Rome." However, Crassus died in the Battle of Carrhae during the invasion of the Parthian Empire in 53. After his death, Caesar and Pompey began to grow apart, and Pompey joined forces with Caesar's political opponents.

Caesar was leading the armies against the Gauls at that time, but upon his return to Rome, he was asked to give the army back to the state. If he didn't, he wouldn't be permitted another term as consul. But this act would leave Caesar defenseless, so he chose civil war over giving up his military command. Caesar's civil war started in 49 when the Senate proclaimed him to be an enemy of the state, and the senators worked closely with his former friend Pompey to bring him down. Pompey received dictatorial powers from the Senate to be able to move against Caesar freely, but his army was young and had yet to be tested.

On January 10, Caesar's army, which was made out of veterans, crossed the river Rubicon, which represented the legal border of Roman Italy. By crossing this natural border, Caesar directly broke the Roman law that stated no army was allowed beyond the Rubicon. He reached Rome not facing any major challenges, and his fast progress made Pompey and most of the Senate flee Rome and find refuge in Greece. Caesar went after Pompey but was initially defeated, only to rise victorious in the Battle of Pharsalus in 48. Pompey had to run again, this time to Egypt, where he was assassinated by King Ptolemy XIII's advisors in 48.

Pompey's death did not end the civil war, as his supporters continued fighting Caesar. However, ultimately, Caesar was victorious and defeated the Pompeian forces at the Battle of Munda in 45. Finally, the order was restored, and the civil war ended. Caesar took hold of the dictatorship and the tribunate, which gave him the power to veto the Senate. Caesar was the primary figure in Rome, and his power reached far, influencing enemies as well as allies. His political opponents were afraid that he was destroying the republic and that it was only a matter of time until he would crown himself as the emperor. Caesar had no intention of becoming an emperor by title and officially refused a diadem during the Lupercalia festival celebrations. It is considered that the offering of the diadem to Caesar and his refusal were staged in order to appease the people of Rome. At that time, Caesar continued his relationship with Cleopatra VII, the queen of Egypt, who was visiting Rome with their son, Caesarion.

Julius Caesar was assassinated on March 15, 44. The assassination was organized by dozens of senators, and they were led by Gaius Cassius and Marcus Brutus. Each person involved had various political, economic, or personal reasons to dispose of Caesar, but they all gathered around the common fear of the return of the monarchy if they allowed Caesar to continue having that much power. All the conspirators had to flee Rome because of the threat of retaliation from Caesar's supporters. A new civil war followed, and it destroyed what remained of the Roman Republic and paved the path for the Roman Empire.

Mark Antony, Caesar's lieutenant, and Gaius Octavius, Caesar's adopted son and heir, joined forces and fought against Brutus and Cassius, the latter two committing suicide after their defeat. Together with Marcus Aemilius Lepidus, Caesar's former ally, Octavius and Mark Antony formed the Second Triumvirate in 43. They shared all the powers Caesar used to hold, continuing the tradition of having a powerless Senate. This alliance did not last long as Octavius was too ambitious and turned against his allies, starting a new civil war. At the battle of Actium in 31, Octavius defeated Mark Antony, who had allied himself with Cleopatra. In order to dispose of any possible threat to his throne, he murdered Cleopatra's and Caesar's son, Caesarion, but spared any children she had with Mark Antony. With this victory, Octavius gained the powers of an emperor within the city of Rome. Soon after, he was given the title of Augustus, which symbolized his high status over all the Romans. He became the first emperor of the new Roman Empire, which, when taking into consideration the Eastern Roman Empire, lasted until 1453.

Conclusion – The End of an Age

The beginning of the end of the Hellenistic Age was brought by the intervention of the Roman Empire. The largest contributor to the Roman invasion was probably Philip V's alliance with Hannibal. That act proved to the Romans that the Macedonian dynasties held too much power and had the potential to threaten the republic. As a result, a new policy of weakening the status of the monarchs and the relationships between states and cities was put into place.

The influence of Rome caused a degree of chaos and uncertainty within the Hellenistic states, and decades of plotting and fighting against each other began almost immediately. For generations, the Macedonian families plotted against each other and themselves, significantly weakening their position by losing the support of their own people. Corruption and greed were enough to show the citizens of the Hellenistic world that they needed a new protector. Rome seemed to be the only alternative.

The Greek civilizations were slowly integrated within the Roman Republic, and their position was solidified at the end of the Roman civil war. The decisive strikes that wiped the remnants of the old Macedonian dynasties took place in 31 when Octavian defeated Mark Antony and his Ptolemaic forces, which led to Octavian's capturing of Alexandria and the subsequent suicide of Cleopatra VII in 30, as she would have rather died than be paraded as some prize for Octavian to tout across the lands. With this death, the Hellenistic age ended. However, its memory and spirit would be carried across the centuries by the new Roman imperial system.

References

Austin, M. M. (2011). *The Hellenistic World from Alexander to the Roman Conquest: A Selection of Ancient Sources in Translation.* Cambridge University Press.

Bennett, B., & Roberts, M. (2008). *The Wars of Alexander's Successors, 323-281 BC.* Barnsley, England: Pen & Sword Military.

Cary, M. (1978). *A History of the Greek World: From 323 to 146 B.C.* LONDON: METHUEN.

Green, P. (2008). *Alexander to Actium: The Historical Evolution of the Hellenistic Age.* Berkeley, CA: Univ. of California Press.

Kralli, I. (2017). *The Hellenistic Peloponnese: Interstate Relations - A Narrative and Analytic History, 371-146 BC.* Swansea: The Classical Press of Wales.

Thonemann, P. J. (2016). *The Hellenistic Age.* Oxford: Oxford University Press.

Walbank, F. W. (1992). *The Hellenistic World.* London: Fontana Press.

Check out more books by Captivating History

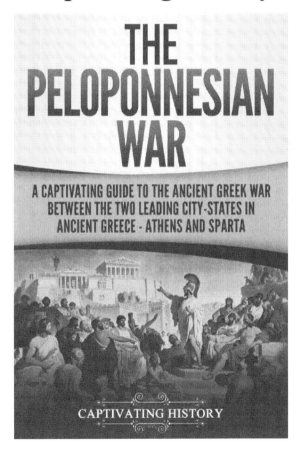

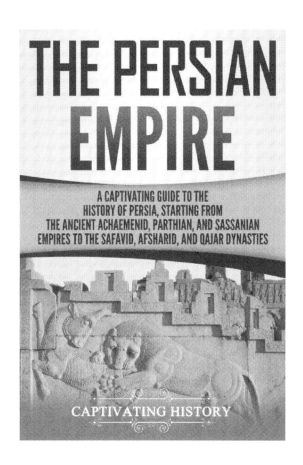

48496461R00078

Printed in Poland
by Amazon Fulfillment
Poland Sp. z o.o., Wrocław